Woman
Blessed

Destiny Image Books by T.D. Jakes

Woman, Thou Art Loosed! (20th Anniversary Expanded Edition)

Woman, Thou Art Loosed Guided Journal

Woman, Thou Art Blessed

Woman, Thou Art Blessed Guided Journal

Release Your Destiny, Release Your Anointing: Expanded Edition

Healing, Blessings, and Freedom: 365-Day Devotional & Journal

Insights to Help You Survive the Peaks and Valleys

It's Time to Reveal What God Longs to Heal

Can You Stand to Be Blessed?

Healing the Wounds of the Past

T.D. Jakes Devotional and Journal

Strength for Every Moment

Hope for Every Moment

Wisdom from T.D. Jakes

Why? Because You Are Anointed!

When Power Meets Potential

God Longs to Heal You

T.D. Jakes Speaks on Power

Water in the Wilderness

Power for Living

Strength to Stand

Are You Ready?

The Harvest

Unlocked

Identity

Woman thou art Blessed

A Guided Gratitude Journal

T.D. JAKES

DESTINY IMAGE® PUBLISHERS, INC.

P.O. Box 310, Shippensburg, PA 17257-0310

"Publishing cutting-edge prophetic resources to supernaturally empower the body of Christ"

This book and all other Destiny Image and Destiny Image Fiction books are available at Christian bookstores and distributors worldwide.

For more information on foreign distributors, call 717-532-3040.

Reach us on the Internet: www.destinyimage.com.

ISBN 13 TP: 978-0-7684-7458-9

For Worldwide Distribution, Printed in the U.S.A.

1 2 3 4 5 6 7 8 / 27 26 25 24 23

Introduction

B ishop T.D. Jakes has influenced millions worldwide to give their love and lives to Jesus. His Holy Spirit-inspired messages are empowering and encouraging—resulting in day after day and year after year of blessings and miracles.

The content in this guided journal has been specially selected from one of Bishop Jakes's most inspiring books, *Woman, Thou Art Blessed,* which has touched people around the world who were searching for more than just religious platitudes.

Similar to Bishop Jakes's *Woman, Thou Art Loosed Guided Journal,* this guided journal includes comments and questions to stir up buried events or situations that should be dug up and dealt with— whatever may be holding you back spiritually, physically, relationally, mentally, and/or emotionally from being who God created you to be.

On every page are valuable Scripture passages pertaining to a lavish lifestyle in Christ, godly wisdom from Bishop Jakes, as well as "thought prompts"—all designed to illuminate anything that may have been preventing your true, unique self from shining through.

This guided journal may be used independently or in combination with the book *Woman, Thou Art Blessed.* Jesus Christ brought with Him abundant-living blessings from Heaven for all of God's children for every area of your life. Divine purpose and promises are yours for the asking.

God enables you to make the radical changes necessary to rock your world with His blessings.

A few of the numerous Scriptures throughout the Bible that declare God's promise of blessings include:

> *You* [God] *prepare a feast for me in the presence of my enemies. You honor me by anointing my head with oil. My cup overflows with blessings* (Psalm 23:5 NLT).

When they walk through the Valley of Weeping, it will become a place of refreshing springs. The autumn rains will clothe it with blessings (Psalm 84:6 NLT).

You [God] go before me and follow me. You place your hand of blessing on my head (Psalm 139:5 NLT).

For I will pour out water to quench your thirst and to irrigate your parched fields. And I will pour out my Spirit on your descendants, and my blessing on your children (Isaiah 44:3 NLT).

From his [God's] abundance we have all received one gracious blessing after another (John 1:16 NLT).

The apostles testified powerfully to the resurrection of the Lord Jesus, and God's great blessing was upon them all (Acts 4:33 NLT).

When he [Barnabas] arrived and saw this evidence of God's blessing, he was filled with joy, and he encouraged the believers to stay true to the Lord (Acts 11:23 NLT).

This interactive journal allows you to delve into a world of blessings where God's abundant love showers you with joy and grace. You will feel His mercy and see His wisdom at every page turn. Considering and answering the prompts will stir, motivate, strengthen, and give you pause for intentional, deep reflection—venturing into previously unknown spiritual realms.

Journeying with the Holy Spirit, you will explore a beautiful space that only God could create, especially for you.

Get ready to experience a new life in Christ as you peel away the troubles and trauma to uncover the blessings waiting for you and freely given to you by your heavenly Father. Abundant life and blessings galore await you!

Your Guided Journal

Your Purpose, His Promise

But as many as received Him, to them He gave the right to become children of God, to those who believe in His name (John 1:12 NKJV).

God placed His divine purpose and prophetic promises in you at creation. They are still within you, ready to burst forth. If the past is still haunting you, fear not. If you feel as if you're in the fire, fear not. There is a fourth Man in the fire, and He wants to set you free (see Daniel 3:19-28). As a child of God, the fire only burns the ties that bind you. It might get hot, but God always provides a way to escape.

🌸 In my mind, being a child of God means having to give up _____ and submit to His _____.

I know in my heart and my head that my heavenly Father:

_____

🌸 When life gets tough, my first reaction is to:

Your Potential

> *I knew you before I formed you in your mother's womb.*
> *Before you were born I set you apart and appointed you*
> *as my prophet to the nations* (Jeremiah 1:5 NLT).

All types of potential were locked into your spirit before birth. For the Christian, transformation at its optimum is the outworking of the internal. Daughter, you house the prophetic power of God. Every word of your personal prophetic destiny is inside you. He has ordained you to be! He gives us the power to become who we are eternally and internally. His power is not intimidated by your circumstances. It is important to realize that you are able to accomplish what others could not only because God gave you the grace to do so. You are empowered by God to reach and accomplish goals that transcend human limitations!

🌿 Knowing now that I "house the prophetic power of God," am I humbled? Afraid? Overwhelmed? Or am I:

🌿 To discover what God's will and goals for my life are, I will:

🌿 To reach and accomplish God's goals for my life, I will immediately:

🌿 And over the long term I will:

Like Jesus

For God knew his people in advance, and he chose them to become like his Son, so that his Son would be the firstborn among many brothers and sisters (Luke 13:13 NLT).

God has predestined you to shape up into a picture of Christ on earth. Christ is the firstborn of a huge family of siblings who all bear a striking resemblance to their Father. God presses the oil of His anointing out of your life. When you forsake your will in order to be shaped into a clearer picture of Christ, you will see little drops of oil coming out in your walk and work for God. In short, He predestined pressing in your life, and as you are pressed, you gradually conform to the image of your predestined purpose.

🌿 In what ways do I resemble Jesus:

🌿 In what ways can I attempt to reflect Jesus in my everyday walk with Him:

Agony, But Not Defeat

And being in agony, He prayed more earnestly. Then His sweat became like great drops of blood falling down to the ground (Luke 22:44 NKJV).

God predestined you to be conformed to the image of Jesus, a beloved child of God. Jesus went to the garden of Gethsemane and sweat drops of blood in fervent prayer before His Father—laying down His will for the Father's salvation of humankind. The standards of this world might say that adversity means you did something wrong, but God has a different standard. He uses adversity, even agony, to press you and develop your character for ultimate victory.

❧ Am I willing to lay down my wants for the needs of others:

❧ How developed is my character according to God's standard? The world's standard?

Toss It

...throw off your old sinful nature and your former way of life, which is corrupted by lust and deception. Instead, let the Spirit renew your thoughts and attitudes. Put on your new nature, created to be like God—truly righteous and holy (Ephesians 4:22-24 NLT).

No matter what has misidentified you in the past, in God is the power to be transformed into His likeness. Everyone is affected by circumstances. Maybe negative words are still ringing in your ears and your self-perception is still suffering. Fear not, daughter! The Holy Spirit knows how to renew your mind and bring you to the place of maturity where your self-image comes directly from Him—and you can see the blessings He has for you.

🌺 Sometimes I feel so defeated that I can't even…

🌺 But when I open my heart to the Holy Spirit, I feel as if I could…

The Promise Keeper

> And the Lord said, "That's right, and it means that I am watching, and I will certainly carry out all my plans" (Jeremiah 1:12 NLT).

God is sovereign. If He decrees something, it will surely come to pass. That doesn't stop the evil one from trying to delay the fulfillment of what God has said, but he can't stop it from happening. Your blessing may not come in the way you thought it would. It may not come through the person you thought it would. But if God said it, then rest assured it cannot be denied.

Sometimes we need to let go of our ideas of how things should be to see where He's moving. If things didn't go according to plan, ask God for His perspective. Ask Him if there is anything you need to let go of—perhaps a past disappointment—so you can see that He indeed is the Promise Keeper.

🌿 Knowing that God is always watching over me brings me to a place of:

🌿 Today I accept the truth that God keeps His word and His promises—which will change my life in these ways:

Be Confident

being confident of this very thing, that He who has begun a good work in you will complete it until the day of Jesus Christ (Philippians 1:6 NKJV).

Do you feel like some things in your life didn't go how you hoped they would? Maybe you have experienced a painful loss. Or maybe a dream or vision feels dead. Those circumstances can bring us to bleak despair, but nothing catches God by surprise. He knows everything that has happened and will happen in your life. You can trust Him even if things look messy or out of control. God will find a way to bless you when you call on Him and are confident that He has your back.

🌿 On a scale from 1 (least) to 10 (best), how confident am I overall that my life is on the right track:

Spiritually _____

Emotionally _____

Relationally _____

Financially _____

🌿 If not a 10 in each, what can I do to raise each score to a 10:

Like Wildflowers

Our days on earth are like grass; like wildflowers, we bloom and die (Psalm 103:15 NLT).

W e come into this world fully cognizant of the fact that we have a limited amount of time. We don't live here for very long before we are confronted with the cold realities of death. From the loss of a goldfish to the death of a grandparent, all parents find themselves saddled with the responsibility of explaining why the pet or the person will not be coming back anymore. Yet what disturbs me most is not the quantity of life, but the quality of life. Simply stated, when death comes to push me through its window from time into eternity, I want to feel as though I accomplished something worthwhile. I want to feel that my life made some positive statement.

🌺 Death is a topic I would rather not:

🌺 Death is a topic I know I should:

Fresh Hope

> [Eve] *bore a son and named him Seth, "For God has appointed another seed for me instead of Abel, whom Cain killed"* (Genesis 4:25 NKJV).

Loss is very real and all of us will have to walk through it at certain points in life. The emotions Eve must have gone through were legitimate and valid. One of her sons was gone forever. The other was convicted of murder, which isn't anyone's dream for their child (see Genesis 4). The heartbreak would have gone very deep. If you've suffered loss or disappointment, take the time to grieve. Let God meet you in that situation and heal your heart, beloved, but don't stay there. God has promises over your life that will not be denied. Let Him take you by the hand and lead you into the next season. Spend time inviting the Holy Spirit into your disappointment or loss today. Ask God for fresh hope for your good and beautiful future.

🌿 I know deep down that God is able to:

🌿 Have I ever really invited the Holy Spirit into my life during times of loss:

Hold On!

He gives strength to the weary and increases the power of the weak (Isaiah 40:29 NIV).

The saddest scenario I can imagine would be to face death's rattling call and wonder what would have happened if I had tried harder. It would be terrible to look back over your life and see that the many times you thought your request was denied, it was actually only delayed. Life will always present broken places, places of struggle and conflict. If you have a divine purpose and life has put you on hold, hang on! Stay in prayer. If you believe as I do, then it's worth the wait to receive your answer and blessing from the Lord.

🌿 When I look back over my life so far, there have been times when I:

🌿 How many broken places and struggles and conflicts am I facing right now that can be mended and settled by just resting in God's peace? I will absorb Philippians 4:7 into my spirit by:

It's All About Faith and Trust

I waited patiently for the Lord to help me, and he turned to me and heard my cry. He lifted me out of the pit of despair, out of the mud and the mire. He set my feet on solid ground and steadied me as I walked along. He has given me a new song to sing, a hymn of praise to our God. Many will see what he has done and be amazed. They will put their trust in the Lord (Psalm 40:1-3 NLT).

The real test of faith and trusting God is in facing the silence of being on hold. Those are the suspended times of indecision. Have you ever faced those times when your life seemed stagnant? Have you felt you were on the verge of something phenomenal, that you were waiting for that particular breakthrough that seemed to be taunting you by making you wait? All of us have faced days that seemed as though God had forgotten us. These are the moments that feel like eternity. These silent coaches take your patience into strenuous calisthenics. Patience gets a workout when God's answer is no answer. In other words, God's answer is not always yes or no; sometimes He says, "Not now!"

🌿 It's hard for me to be patient because:

🌺 While waiting on God's answer, I can fill the silence with songs and praise so that:

God Doesn't Forget

God is not unjust; he will not forget your work and the love you have shown him as you have helped his people and continue to help them (Hebrews 6:10 NIV).

You feel a deep sense of contentment when you know God has not forgotten you. When working with people, we often must remind them that we are still there. They seem to readily forget who you are or what you did. God doesn't! Don't confuse your relationship with Him with your relationship with people. In Hebrews 6, God says, through Paul, that He does not forget. We must learn God's timing. He synchronizes His answers and blessings to accomplish His purpose. God simply doesn't forget.

🌿 Too many times I feel alone and forgotten, which makes me:

🌿 Working with people isn't always easy, so I:

Road Trip!

> *God said to Noah…"Build a large boat from cypress wood and waterproof it with tar, inside and out. Then construct decks and stalls throughout its interior"* (Genesis 6:13-14 NLT).

Do you remember long road trips as a child? Or maybe you have children and car rides feel eternally long. Life can feel like that too when we're waiting for something we really want but don't have yet. Children ask the question "Are we there yet?" repeatedly until finally the destination is reached. We can be like that too, continuously reminding God that we are still down here waiting. But, my daughter, God did not forget you. You might feel like life is stagnant and you have no answers, but God is never stagnant. He is always working on your heart and orchestrating situations to fulfill His purposes in you and for you. Rest in Him and ask Him to teach you about His perfect timing.

🌱 Am I prone to nag God about my life?

🌱 How impatient am I to get to my destination in my timing?

God Remembers

> *God remembered Noah, and every living thing, and all the animals that were with him in the ark. And God made a wind to pass over the earth, and the waters subsided* (Genesis 8:1 NKJV).

I will never forget the time I went through a tremendous struggle. I thought it was an emergency. I thought I had to have an answer right then. I learned that God isn't easily spooked by what I call an emergency. While struggling in my heart to understand why He had not more readily answered my request, I stumbled upon a verse in the Bible that brought streams into my desert.

The first three words were all I needed: *God remembered Noah.* I still quote them from time to time. When you realize that God knows where you are and that He will get back to you in time—what peace, what joy, what blessing!

🌿 I am guilty of making trivial molehills into emergency mountains. From now on I will:

🌿 Right now, peace, joy, and blessing sound so:

Real Ammunition

Jesus Christ is the same yesterday, today, and forever (Hebrews 13:8 NLT).

Before Noah ran out of resources and provisions, God remembered him! The Lord knows where you are and He knows how much you have left in reserve. Just before you run out, God will send the wind to blow back the waters of impossibility and provide for you. I can't begin to describe the real ammunition I received out of those three powerful words: *God remembered Noah*. When I read them, I knew God also remembered me. I too need ministry to keep my attitude from falling while I wait on the manifestation of the promises of God. Sometimes very simplistic reminders that God is still sovereign bring great joy to my heart. The comforting Spirit of God calms my fears every time He reminds me that God never forgets.

🌿 I will make a serious effort to watch for "real ammunition" phrases and verses when reading God's Word so I can:

🌿 Calming my fears is hard for me at times because:

Rain, Rain, Go Away

The rain continued to fall for forty days and forty nights (Genesis 7:12 NLT).

God is working at every moment, but there is a much bigger picture than what we see. In Noah's day, God had a very specific plan that made no sense in the natural realm. Noah had to build a giant boat for his family and all the animal species. Imagine what people must have said about him as he worked. He probably felt a little crazy. Then it rained for 40 days. Noah and his family were in the ark for almost a year! I bet they wondered if those storms would ever end. Maybe they felt forgotten, but then those three words: *But God remembered Noah.* Oh, beloved, no matter how long the storm has been, God remembers. He will blow back the waters and make a way. Ask Him for a glimpse into eternity today.

🌿 Just one rainy day makes me feel as if:

🌿 When I put myself in the place of Noah when reading chapters 7 and 8 in Genesis, I believe, trust, and have faith in God because He is:

Roaring Windstorm

> *On the day of Pentecost all the believers were meeting together in one place. Suddenly, there was a sound from heaven like the roaring of a mighty windstorm, and it filled the house where they were sitting* (Acts 2:1-2 NLT).

God's records are so complete that the hairs on your head are numbered (see Matthew 10:30). They are not just counted. Counted would mean He simply knows how many. No, they are numbered, meaning He knows which hair is in your comb! How much more would God watch over you if He already watches the numerical order of your hair? When Noah had been held up long enough to accomplish what was necessary for his good, God sent the wind. There is a wind that comes from the Presence of God. It blows back the hindrances and dries the ground beneath your feet. The wind of the Holy Spirit often comes as a sign to you from the control tower. You have been cleared for a landing! Whenever the breath of the Almighty breathes a fresh anointing on you, it is a divine indication of a supernatural deliverance.

🌿 What comes immediately to my mind when I read Acts 2:1-2 is:

I am waiting—patiently—for a supernatural deliverance from:

Holy Spirit's Mighty Wind

And suddenly there came a sound from heaven, as of a rushing mighty wind, and it filled the whole house where they were sitting (Acts 2:2 NKJV).

Regardless of any obstacle in your life, there is a wind from God that can bring you victory. Let the wind of the Lord blow down every spirit of fear and heaviness that would cause you to give up on what God has promised you. The description of the Holy Spirit says He is as "a rushing mighty wind." For every mighty problem in your life, there is a mighty rushing wind! A normal wind can be blocked out. If you close the door and lock the windows, the wind just passes over without changing the building. But if the wind is a mighty rushing wind, it will blow down the door and break in the windows. A gusty wind from the Lord is too strong to be controlled. It will blow back the Red Sea. It will roll back the Jordan River. It will blow dry the wet, marshy, flooded lands as in the days of Noah. God's wind is still victorious against every current event in your life.

🌱 When I give the Holy Spirit full rein to blow through every door and window of myself, I am confident that the spirit of fear and heaviness will:

The Holy Spirit will replace the spirit of fear and heaviness with:

Divided Waters

Then Moses stretched out his hand over the sea; and the Lord caused the sea to go back by a strong east wind all that night, and made the sea into dry land, and the waters were divided (Exodus 14:21 NKJV).

Throughout the Bible, the Red Sea is mentioned as a reference point to God's miraculous, delivering power. The Israelites were being chased by the Egyptian armies. When they got to the Red Sea, they were terrified. Then God parted the waters. They walked through on dry ground and their enemies drowned. God is mighty to save and strong to deliver. His ways don't usually look the way we expect. When our enemies are chasing us down, fear is very real. Maybe that is why God gave us many examples of His deliverance. Read Exodus chapter 14 and let it stir up your faith in God's mighty power to deliver you. If you are facing an impossibility, ask God to blow the wind of His Holy Spirit and make a way through the waters and into blessings.

❧ Right now, or in the past, I have stood facing a tidal wave of troubles that caused me to:

❧ I remember a time when fear kept me from:

The Greatest Investment

And all the believers met together in one place and shared everything they had. They sold their property and possessions and shared the money with those in need (Acts 2:44-45 NLT).

There is a difference in the emotional makeup of a child who has had a substantial deposit of affection and affirmation. Great affirmation occurs when someone invests into our personhood. I believe that people are the greatest investments in the world. A wonderful bond exists between the person who invests and the one in whom the investment is made. This bond evolves from the heart of anyone who recognizes the investment was made before the person accomplished the goal. Anyone will invest in a sure success, but aren't we grateful when someone supports us when we are somewhat of a risk? It is impossible to discuss the value of investing in people and not find ourselves worshiping God—what a perfect picture of investment. God is the major stockholder. No matter who He later uses to enhance our characters, we need to remember the magnitude of God's investment in our lives.

🌿 Do I see people as investments for God's Kingdom or annoyances?

Has someone valued me enough to invest time and advice into my life? Did I accepted this gift? Have I extended investment time and advice into someone's life?

Risky Investments

They worshiped together at the Temple each day, met in homes for the Lord's Supper, and shared their meals with great joy and generosity—all the while praising God and enjoying the goodwill of all the people. And each day the Lord added to their fellowship those who were being saved (Acts 2:46-47 NLT).

God created us for relationship and those relationships enhance our life. We fulfill our purposes together. Whether or not you've had nurturing, affection, and affirmation from people, remember that Jesus paid the highest price for your life. He believes in you that much. He says you are worth the risk and you're worth investing in. In the body of Christ, we have the opportunity to call out each other's potential and help each other discover inner strengths. Investing in people who are "risky" can have the most impact. Like all high-risk investments, there is possibility for a great return. God knows what He placed in each person. Ask Him to show you who is in need of your investment.

🌿 Who can I affirm and nurture as they work toward their potential?

🌿 Acts 2:46-47 exudes a genuine feeling of joy and fellowship and makes me smile and wonder…

🌿 Does my church or fellowship with Christians bring this same feeling? How can I bring this atmosphere into my relationships?

Pure Gold

He knows where I am going. And when he tests me, I will come out as pure as gold (Job 23:10 NLT).

God is serious about producing the change in our lives that will glorify Him and bring us blessings. He will fight to protect the investment He has placed in your life. What a comfort it is to know that the Lord has a vested interest in my deliverance. He has more than just concern for me. God has begun the necessary process of cultivating what He has invested in my life. Have you ever stopped to think that it was God's divine purpose that kept you afloat when others capsized beneath the load of life? Look at Job; he knew that God had an investment in his life that no season of distress could eradicate. Whenever you see someone shining with the kind of brilliancy that enables God to look down and see Himself, you are looking at someone who has been through the furnace of affliction.

🌿 Can I really say that I've been through the furnace of affliction?

🌿 Can I really say that God can look down and see Himself in me?

The Refiner

He will sit like a refiner of silver, burning away the dross. He will purify the Levites, refining them like gold and silver, so that they may once again offer acceptable sacrifices to the Lord (Malachi 3:3 NLT).

If you want to shine brightly, you have to go through the fire that purifies your character and commitment. God knows exactly what you need to achieve your full potential. He invested in your salvation, and now He continuously invests in your life. The fires He brings you through are for your good. And He has a vested interest in your deliverance. The same God who leads you into the fire is faithful to bring you out again, purified. Can you look back on your life and see the good that came out of difficult seasons? Did you learn something about God? Did your character change? If there are any areas of your life that feel under fire right now, ask God to give you clarity and assurance that He has a purpose.

🌿 These several areas seem to be under fire right now in my life:

🌿 Lord God, please give me a clear understanding of these troubles and how they will benefit me in the long run for Your purpose and glory.

The Fourth Person

Then King Nebuchadnezzar was astonished; and he rose in haste and spoke, saying to his counselors, "Did we not cast three men bound into the midst of the fire?" They answered and said to the king, "True, O king." "Look!" he answered, "I see four men loose, walking in the midst of the fire; and they are not hurt, and the form of the fourth is like the Son of God" (Daniel 3:24-25 NKJV).

Remember the story of the three Hebrew boys in the fiery furnace? When the wicked king placed them in the fire, he thought the fire would burn them. He didn't know that when you belong to God, the fire only burns the ties that bind you. People have said that God took the heat out of the furnace. That is not true. Consider the soldiers who threw the Hebrews into the fire—they were burned to death at the door! There was plenty of heat in the furnace. God, however, controls the boundaries. Have you ever gone through a dilemma that should have scorched every area of your life and yet you survived the pressure? If yes, then you know that He is Lord over the fire!

🌿 Fire can refine and it can also kill—knowing that God is the Lord over every fire burning in my life gives me the confidence to:

🌸 Trusting God to get me through each fire means:

Real Faith

> *"Look!" Nebuchadnezzar shouted. "I see four men, unbound, walking around in the fire unharmed!"* (Daniel 3:25 NLT).

It has been suggested that if you walk in the Spirit, you won't have to contend with the fire. Real faith doesn't mean you won't go through the fire. Real faith simply means that when you pass through the fire, He will be with you. This thought brings you to an unusual reality. In most cases, if I told you that tomorrow you would be burned alive, but not to worry because I would be in the fire with you, my presence in the dilemma would provide no comfort at all. Yet the presence of the Lord can turn a burning inferno into a walk in the park! The Bible says a fourth person was in the fire, and so the three Hebrews were able to walk around unharmed in it (see Daniel 3). King Nebuchadnezzar was astonished when he saw them overcome what had destroyed other men. If you believe God, you can walk in what other people burn in. Remember, the fire only burns the ties that bind you.

🌿 I realize that only God can walk with me through the fires when life seems too...

When others around me are burning in self-destructive fiery furnaces, I will cling to…

Don't Panic

> *So be strong and courageous! Do not be afraid and do not panic before them. For the Lord your God will personally go ahead of you. He will neither fail you nor abandon you* (Deuteronomy 31:6 NLT).

Faith does not give you an easy life. More often, the exact opposite is true. The more faith we have, the more fire we can endure. He doesn't spare us from moments that require radical faith and great courage. Moses told the Israelites to be strong and of good courage. He reminded them that God would be with them and never fail them or forsake them. God goes with us through the Red Sea. He goes into the blazing furnace and preserves our lives. Even in death, Jesus went before us and conquered hell and the grave. He truly is Lord over the fire. What if God asked you to walk right into a scary and impossible situation? Would you be ready to follow? Remember, He will be right by your side, ready to bless you abundantly.

🌿 I know people who have (or I have) experienced panic attacks and the feeling is:

🌿 My strength and courage waver whenever I:

Feet of Fire

Then I turned to see the voice that spoke with me. And having turned I saw seven golden lampstands, and in the midst of the seven lampstands One like the Son of Man, clothed with a garment down to the feet and girded about the chest with a golden band. His head and hair were white like wool, as white as snow, and His eyes like a flame of fire; His feet were like fine brass, as if refined in a furnace, and His voice as the sound of many waters (Revelation 1:12-15 NKJV).

John says that Jesus' voice was like the sound of rushing waters and that His feet looked as if burned by the fire. What a comfort to realize that Jesus knows what it feels like to be in the fire.

I cannot guarantee that you will not face terrifying situations if you believe God. But I can declare that if you face life with Christ's presence, the effects of the circumstance will be drastically altered. Rest assured that God knows your fiery path to victory. He can heal your blistered feet. Thank God for the smoldering feet of our Lord that run swiftly to meet His children in need. If you are in a fiery trial, know that it is your faith that is on trial. If you are to overcome the dilemma, it will not be by your feelings, but by your faith. If faith doesn't deliver you from it—it will surely deliver you through it.

🌺 Ephesians 6:16 tells me that the *"shield of faith"* quenches the fiery darts of the devil. Therefore I will hold my shield high and...

My Deliverer's feet have been burned. He knows what it feels like to be in the fire with me. With this knowledge, I will forever…

By Faith

By faith these people overthrew kingdoms, ruled with justice, and received what God had promised them. They shut the mouths of lions, quenched the flames of fire, and escaped death by the edge of the sword. Their weakness was turned to strength. They became strong in battle and put whole armies to flight (Hebrews 11:33-34 NLT).

The fanaticism of some faith theology has intimidated many Christians from faith concepts as they relate to the promises and blessings of God. Yet faith is such a key issue for the Christian that the people of the early Church were simply called "believers" in recognition of their great faith. One thing we need to do is understand the distinctions of faith. Faith cannot alter purpose; it only acts as an agent to assist in fulfilling the predetermined purpose of God. If God's plan requires that we suffer certain opposition to accomplish His purpose, then faith becomes the vehicle to persevere and delivers us through the test. On the other hand, the enemy afflicts the believer in an attempt to abort the purpose of God. Faith is a night watchman sent to guard the purpose of God. Faith delivers us out of the hand of the enemy—the enemy is anything that hinders the purpose of God in our lives.

❧ How much faith do I have that I will fulfill my godly purpose in this life I have on earth?

How much faith do I have that I will be rescued from the enemies of procrastination, fear, lack of motivation, sin, selfishness, and the like?

Cruise-Control Living

> *Store your treasures in heaven, where moths and rust*
> *cannot destroy, and thieves do not break in and steal*
> (Matthew 6:20 NLT).

Hebrews chapter 11 discusses at length the definition of faith, shares the deeds of faith, and discusses the perseverance of faith. There are distinctions of faith as well, such as faith that escapes peril and overcomes obstacles. Christianity's foundation is not built upon elite mansions, stocks and bonds, or sports cars and cruise-control living. All these things are wonderful if God chooses to bless you with them. However, to make finances the symbol of faith is ridiculous. The Church is built on the backs of people who withstood discomfort for a cause. These heroes were not the end but the means whereby God was glorified. Some of them exhibited their faith through their shadows' healing sick people (see Acts 5:15). Others were martyred for the Kingdom (see Acts 7:59). They also had a brand of faith that seemed to ease the effects, though it didn't alter the cause.

🌿 My idea of cruise-control living is:

🌿 What "brand of faith" or "discomfort for a cause" defines me?

Consuming Fire

> *My old self has been crucified with Christ. It is no longer I who live, but Christ lives in me. So I live in this earthly body by trusting in the Son of God, who loved me and gave himself for me* (Galatians 2:20 NLT).

As the fire of persecution forces us to make deeper levels of commitment, it is so important that our faith be renewed to match our level of commitment. There is a place in God where the fire consumes every other desire but to know the Lord in the power of His resurrection. At this level all other pursuits tarnish and seem worthless in comparison. Perhaps this is what Paul really pressed toward, that place of total surrender. Certainly that is the place I reach toward, which often escapes my grasp, but never my view. Like a child standing on his toes, I reach after a place too high to be touched. I conclude by saying my hands are extended, but my feet are on fire!

🌱 It seems that _____ is competing with my desire for Jesus.

🌱 Am I willing to allow God to purify my heart like gold if it means discomfort?

Second Chances

> *Therefore God also has highly exalted Him and given Him the name which is above every name, that at the name of Jesus every knee should bow, of those in heaven, and of those on earth, and of those under the earth* (Philippians 2:9-10 NKJV).

A good name is a very precious possession, often more lucrative than financial prosperity. If your name is associated with wealth, ministry, scandal, etc., your name soon becomes synonymous with whatever it is most often associated. The dilemma for many people can be put like this: "How can I reverse the image or stigma that has been placed upon my name?" The names of some people are damaged because of past failures and indiscretions. Still others wrestle with the stains of rumors and the disgraceful, damaging defamation of character. Your name is all about your character and identity, not necessarily a literal name. If you want to fulfill your purpose and receive this new name, you have to allow God to transform your character. Then you have to believe in faith whatever God says, even if you don't see it quite yet.

❧ I will bow to the name of Jesus because He is my:

🌸 Dear God, please grant me a second chance so that my name will reflect Your likeness in righteousness, love, mercy, grace, and all the fruits of the Spirit (see Galatians 5:22-23) so that others will…

Who You Are

But as many as received Him, to them He gave the right to become children of God, to those who believe in His name (John 1:12 NKJV).

There is nothing quite like trouble to bring out your true identity. Aren't you glad that you are not limited to public opinion? God's opinion will always prevail. Those three Hebrews came out of the furnace without a trace of smoke. That old king tried to change the name on the package, but he couldn't change the contents of the heart! Can you imagine those boys shouting when they came out? One would say, "Who is like God?" Another would lift his hands and say, "Jehovah is gracious!" The other would smell his clothes, touch his hair, and shout, "Jehovah has helped!"

If you have agonized on bended knees, praying at the altar to know the purpose and will of God for your life, and His answer doesn't line up with your circumstances, then call it what God calls it! The doctor might call it cancer, but if God calls it healed—call it what God calls it. The word of the Lord often stands alone. It has no attorney and it needs no witness. It can stand on its own merit. Whatever He says, you are!

❧ God calls me His child, so I call myself…

Because I believe in His name and I am a child of God, when I walk out of the fire with Him, I will raise my hands and scream, "…

The Living Dead

And you He made alive, who were dead in trespasses and sins (Ephesians 2:1 NKJV).

Sin is separation from relationship with God, but the second death is separation from the presence of God! This concept reminds me of the bone-chilling horror movies we watched as children. By self-inflicted torturous tenacity, corpses would exhume themselves from the grave. These zombies would walk the earth with their hands extended, always searching for but never attaining rest, leaving a trail of victims behind them. That's pretty ghoulish, but it is an accurate description of what sin is: "The Living Dead"! If you're an empty, brokenhearted person walking around always searching for things, tokens of success, I have a word from God for you: "I have come that they [you] may have life" (John 10:10 NIV). Accept Him today! Wake up from the nightmare of the living dead and become a living, loving testimony to the authenticity of the power of God!

🌺 I will invite Jesus into my life right now and for always and forever by…

I have already accepted Jesus as my Lord and Savior, and now I reaffirm my love and commitment to God the Father, the Son, and the Holy Spirit and confirm…

Dead to Sin

> *So you also should consider yourselves to be dead to the power of sin and alive to God through Christ Jesus. Do not let sin control the way you live; do not give in to sinful desires. Do not let any part of your body become an instrument of evil to serve sin. Instead, give yourselves completely to God, for you were dead, but now you have new life. So use your whole body as an instrument to do what is right for the glory of God* (Romans 6:11-13 NLT).

In Paul's day, there was a gruesome, bizarre punishment for murder: the body of the murdered victim was tied to the murderer. Everywhere the murderer went, the corpse did too, for it was attached to him. He could not forget his victim. The odor of decomposing, deteriorating flesh would reek with the stench of rot, contaminating all of life's moments with the ever-present aroma of decadence. That's how Paul felt about the old nature that continued to press in so closely to his existence—always reminding him of things he could neither change nor eradicate. Eventually, for the punished murderer, the dead flesh passed fungus and disease to him until he died. What an agonizing, disgusting way to die. When the apostle Paul realized that his association with his past was affecting his present, he cried out, "O wretched man that I am! Who will deliver me from this body of death?" (Romans 7:24 NKJV).

❦ Is my old nature still hanging on me, distorting my new nature?

I pray that God will reveal any death and decay so together we can remove it permanently from my life and I can live the blessed new life He promised.

Cut the Cord

So now there is no condemnation for those who belong to Christ Jesus. And because you belong to him, the power of the life-giving Spirit has freed you from the power of sin that leads to death (Romans 8:1-2 NLT).

You can no better live with those dead things clinging to you than Paul could. Allow the transforming power of God to rush through your life and cut the cord between you and your past. Whatever you do, remember to get rid of the old body. If the past is over, there is no need for you to walk around with mummies on your back—or should I say, on your mind! This is the time for an epitaph, not a revival. There are some things in life you will want to revive, but not this one. The past is something you want to die. Jesus is the One found worthy of your thoughts and obedience. He can untie you from the past and set you free. Invite Him into every painful place that's still latching on like that dead body. Receive your freedom here and now.

🌿 Sometimes I think I can't move forward, can't shake the troubles of the past—in fact, it seems I dwell on them. Why do I do that?

🌿 Why would I ever choose to live in self-condemnation rather than in the freedom Christ died to give me?

Burial at Sea

Pharaoh's chariots and his army He has cast into the sea; His chosen captains also are drowned in the Red Sea. The depths have covered them; they sank to the bottom like a stone (Exodus 15:4-5 NKJV).

Mark this day as when you put away your nighttime playmates and moved into abundant life. Gather together all those villainous ghosts that desecrate the sanctity of what God would do in your life. Examine them. Cry if need be; scream if necessary—but when the service is over, bury every incident in the freshly turned soil from God's Word. God has delivered you from playing with dead things. In light of all that you have survived, it is time that the presence of God envelops you in a warm embrace and that the grace of understanding brushes your lips with the kiss of peace in the night. Be like Jesus who said, "It is finished!" (see John 19:30). It is time for that kind of benediction to be said in your life. Allow the God of all grace to give you the final rights that forever exorcise the dead from their secret place of intimate contact with you. You have the power, so bid those old ghosts good-bye. Their grasp is broken, and you will see them no more.

🌿 I declare death to sin and sorrow right now when I…

Into a heavy metal casket I toss my enemies and into the deepest sea I shove it from…

Joyful Mornings

> *For his anger lasts only a moment, but his favor lasts a lifetime! Weeping may last through the night, but joy comes with the morning* (Psalm 30:5 NLT).

Since we have succeeded in destroying our harmful relationships with the past, let's deal with all the side effects from our previous infidelities. These offsprings of another time when we were less spiritually mature cannot be allowed to exist in us. For instance, jealousy is the child of low self-esteem. There is always tiny suicide wrapped in a blanket hiding in the shadows, born in the heart of a person who has been lying in bed with despair or guilt. There are people who habitually lie because fantasy seems more exciting than reality. Promiscuity, the child of a twisted need, has an insatiable appetite like that of greed's, which devours all it touches. For all this, you weep through the night. But David said that if we could hold out for righteousness, joy comes in the morning.

🌿 When offsprings invade my new life, I will:

🌿 A joyful morning looks to me like:

Regain Control

But thank God! He gives us victory over sin and death through our Lord Jesus Christ (1 Corinthians 15:57).

L et the hungry mouth of failure's offspring meet the dry breast of a Christian who has determined to overcome the past. Allow the joy of the morning light to push away any unwanted partners, curses, or fears that stop you from achieving your goal. These embryos of destruction feed on the fears and insecurities of people who haven't declared their liberty. The parent is dead; you have laid him to rest, but if not destroyed, the residue of early traumas will attach itself to your successes and abort your missions and goals. It nurses itself in your thought life, feeding off your inner struggles and inhibitions. To regain control, feed what you want to live and starve what you want to die! You can literally starve those crying, screaming childhood fears into silence, security, and successful encounters. Why not think positively until every negative thing that is a result of dead issues turns blue and releases its grip on your home and your destiny? You've got the power!

🌿 Am I unintentionally feeding my childhood fears and insecurities? To halt that nourishment, I will immediately begin to:

🌸 I will starve my:

🌸 I will feed my:

Offspring of Peace

Don't worry about anything; instead, pray about every-thing. Tell God what you need, and thank him for all he has done. Then you will experience God's peace, which exceeds anything we can understand. His peace will guard your hearts and minds as you live in Christ Jesus. And now, dear brothers and sisters, one final thing. Fix your thoughts on what is true, and honor-able, and right, and pure, and lovely, and admirable. Think about things that are excellent and worthy of praise (Philippians 4:6-8 NLT).

This Scripture passage from Philippians 4 is incredibly signif-icant wisdom and some wonderful food for thought. We see that prayer produces the offspring of peace. This isn't just any peace; it is the peace of God that stands guard over our spirits and hearts, keep-ing us from hysteria in a crisis. People who are filled with excellence achieve that excellence by the thoughts they have about themselves and about the world around them. Thoughts are powerful. They feed the seeds of greatness in our minds. They also can nurse the negative inse-curities that limit us and exempt us from greatness. There is a virtue that comes from tranquil, peaceful thoughts that build positive charac-ter in the heart. As a rule, people who are cynical and vicious tend to be unsuccessful. If they are successful, they don't really feel their success because their cynicism robs from them the sweet taste of reward.

❧ I don't really pray as often as I know I should because…

I would describe the peace of God as…

Secret Thoughts

> *Finally, brothers and sisters, whatever is true, whatever is noble, whatever is right, whatever is pure, whatever is lovely, whatever is admirable—if anything is excellent or praiseworthy—think about such things* (Philippians 4:8 NIV).

Thoughts are secrets hidden behind quick smiles and professional veneers. They are within a private world that others cannot invade. None of us would be comfortable with having all our thoughts played aloud for the whole world to hear. Yet our thoughts can accurately forecast approaching success or failure. No one can hear God think, but we can feel the effects of His thoughts toward us. Like sprouts emerging from enriched soil, our words and eventually our actions push through the fertilized fields of our innermost thoughts. Like our Creator, we deeply affect others by our thoughts toward them—blessing them blesses us.

🌿 I must admit that my thoughts are not always true, noble, right, pure, lovely, admirable, excellent, or praiseworthy. I will strive to "think about such things" more often by:

🌸 Too many of my thoughts are just emotional garbage and don't mean anything. I will start right now to intentionally change my way of thinking toward God's way that brings peace of mind. My first thought is about…

Calloused Hands

Hear my cry for mercy as I call to you for help, as I lift up my hands toward your Most Holy Place (Psalm 28:2 NLT).

In the special moments when thankful hearts and hands lifted in praise come into corporate levels of expression with memories of what could have happened had God not intervened, we find our real ministry. Above all titles and professions, every Christian is called to be a worshiper. We are a royal priesthood that might have become extinct had the mercy of the Lord not arrested the villainous horrors of the enemy. Calloused hands are raised in praise—hands that tell a story of struggle, whether spiritual or natural. These holy hands that we raise unto the Lord are the hands of people who, like Jonah, have lived through a personal hell. Who could better thank the Lord than the oppressed who were delivered by the might of a loving God whose love is tempered with the necessary ability to provoke change?

🌿 Sometimes I feel self-conscious when raising my hands in church. I think this is because I:

When worshiping at home it is easy to raise my hands in praise and to dance before my Lord, as David did in 2 Samuel 6:14. Why is it different when I'm in church?

Oh, So Worthy

He alone is your God, the only one who is worthy of your praise, the one who has done these mighty miracles that you have seen with your own eyes (Deuteronomy 10:21 NLT).

There are so many reasons to praise God. He is worthy of our worship. Before any other purpose or calling He has for us, we are called to be worshipers, priests before Him. This is a lifelong calling, an expression of gratitude and acknowledgment of who He is and all He has done for us. Praising God also drowns out the voice of the enemy. It reminds us of the truth and brings us back to peace, just like in the Philippians 4 passage. Praise is a key to transforming our mind. Play your favorite worship song and bring glory to the Lord today and every day. Lift your holy hands, calloused as they may be, and thank God that your past is gone and your future is bright and beautiful.

🌿 My favorite worship song is _____ because it _____.

🌿 My favorite place and way to worship God are:

Unresolved Heart Issues

Blessed are the pure in heart: for they shall see God (Matthew 5:8 KJV).

If a worshiper has many unresolved issues on her heart, how can she see God? Obstacles keep us seeking the wisdom of people rather than the wisdom of God, which makes us feel insecure while we wait for an answer. Let's clean out our hearts so we will hear, worship, and experience God in a new dimension. Clean out every thought that hinders the peace and power of God. A pure heart is the prerequisite necessary to see God in His fullest sense. How can I see God who cannot be detected in my vision's periphery? Jesus taught that a pure heart could see God. No wonder David cried out, "Create in me a clean heart, O God…" in Psalm 51:10 NKJV. Don't carry around what God wants you to discard. Give your heart a laxative and get rid of "every weight, and the sin which so easily ensnares us" (Hebrews 12:1 NKJV)! What God wants to unveil to you are blessings worth the cleaning out.

🌿 When I first read the title of this journal page, I immediately thought of:

🌿 How clean is my heart on a scale from 1 to 10? What do I need to clean out so I can see God clearly?

New Level of Revelation

I cry out to God Most High, to God who will fulfill his purpose for me (Psalm 57:2 NLT).

From time to time when I minister I have a strange awareness of speaking directly to someone. I feel it now. Whoever you are, get ready for a fresh vision and a new move of God. Shake loose from everything that has kept your heart from seeing God. He is showing Himself. He is not hiding! Clean your heart out and clear your mind; He is with you now! Beloved, do not miss out! Be like David, who constantly brought everything in his heart before the Lord. David is the prime example of allowing God into the deepest places, into all of his emotions, from distress to sorrow to rejection to joy and praise. He held nothing back and God met him every time. Cry out to God and let Him take you to a new level of revelation.

🌿 Yes! I will take deliberate steps to deepen my prayers to my heavenly Father, trusting Him with all my cares and concerns—starting right now with…

🌿 Based on Psalm 57:2, my cry out to the God Most High right now is:

A Complaint

> But I have this complaint against you. You don't love me or each other as you did at first! Look how far you have fallen! Turn back to me and do the works you did at first. If you don't repent, I will come and remove your lampstand from its place among the churches (Revelation 2:4-5 NLT).

Years ago, I often built a fire on those cold wintry nights in West Virginia. Gathering wood was a small price to pay once the logs were ignited and that warm, engulfing glow of hot fire reached out from the stove and filled the room with the soothing sound of crackling wood and the slight aroma of fresh fire. On those nights, I stared into the fire and watched it dance gleefully across the wood like children skipping on a hillside. Bursting up into the air, these occasional eruptions of sparks are nature's answer to fireworks, each group of sparks exploding into neon rainbows of splendor. But these flickering lights are soon extinguished in the aftereffects of being separated from their source. I thought, *How many Christians explode into the brilliancy of worship and praise but are soon dark and cold, losing their first fire.* Stay in the fire, my friend, where the other embers can share their heat with you and keep you ablaze! It is the fire of God that will assist you in burning up the offspring, the oddities, and the obstacles of yesteryear.

🌿 Can I say for certain that I love God and others like I did when I first accepted Jesus as my Lord and Savior?

When and why did that spark fade?

Still My God

> *At about three o'clock, Jesus called out with a loud voice, "Eli, Eli, lema sabachthani?" which means "My God, my God, why have you abandoned me?"* (Matthew 27:46 NLT)

There are times when it is difficult to understand God's methods. There are moments when discerning His will is a frustrating endeavor. Perhaps we have these moments because we haven't been given all the information we need to ascertain His ways as well as His acts. Many times we learn more in retrospect than we do while in the thick of the struggle. I can look over my shoulder at my past and see that the hand of the Lord has been on me all my life. Yet there were times when I felt completely alone and afraid. Even Jesus once cried out to God about feeling alone, as recorded in Matthew 27:46. Suspended on the cross with a bloody, beaten body, He was questioning the acts of God—but He never questioned His relationship with Him. Jesus says in essence, "I don't understand why, but You are still My God!"

I still have some questions about some issues in my past—Holy Spirit, help me see God's hand in those times and bring me resolution. Thank You.

When I cry out to God, I know He will answer because I trust His…

Throes of Life

And I said, "This is my fate; the Most High has turned his hand against me." But then I recall all you have done, O Lord; I remember your wonderful deeds of long ago. They are constantly in my thoughts. I cannot stop thinking about your mighty works (Psalm 77:10-12 NLT).

Generally, we see the workings of God when we look back, but while in the throes of the rumbling winds of life, we are often in search of the Lord. Perhaps we are at our best when we are searching for Him. We have no independence, just raw need. There's no dawdling around with things that have no help or healing. Those are the times we know are jobs for God. If He doesn't help us, we will die. Even if His way seems unfamiliar or confusing, press in to your relationship with Father God. Remember, even Jesus wondered why, but He never questioned His relationship with His Father. Take a moment to just be in God's presence. Leave your wonderings and worries to the side. Just be a child in the arms of your Dad who has the whole world in His hands, including your life.

🌺 I am so thankful for my God who never leaves me or abandons me; in this truth I will:

The most peaceful place in this world is in the arms of my heavenly Father who…

How It Used to Be

*My heart is breaking as I remember how it used to be:
I walked among the crowds of worshipers, leading a
great procession to the house of God, singing for joy
and giving thanks amid the sound of a great celebration!* (Psalm 42:4 NLT).

The search for God is a primary step into worship. God instructs us to seek Him, but not as though He were hiding from us. He is not a child playing hide-and-go-seek. He isn't crouched behind trees giggling while we suffer. The request to seek Him is as much for our benefit as for His. When we seek Him, we make a conscious decision that is necessary for bringing us into the realm of the spiritual. The pursuit of God is rewarding in the development of the seeker's character. Some levels of blessings are never received unless they are diligently sought. Seeking after God often propels Him to perform. There are no manuals that instruct us step by step in the proper way to seek the Lord. Some seek Him quietly, with soft tears falling quietly down a weary face. Others seek Him while walking the sandy beaches, gazing into the swelling currents of an evening tide. Some raise their hands and praise and adore Him with loving expressions of adoration. There are no rules—just that we seek Him with our whole hearts.

🌿 When searching for God, I...

🌿 I seek God not only for my benefit but to give Him the glory and honor He deserves, in light of His...

Spiritually Blind

> *Seek the Lord while you can find him. Call on him now while he is near. Let the wicked change their ways and banish the very thought of doing wrong. Let them turn to the Lord that he may have mercy on them. Yes, turn to our God, for he will forgive generously* (Isaiah 55:6-7 NLT).

We are like blind people when it comes to spiritual issues—we are limited. Like groping fingers extended in the night trying to compensate for the dark, we feel after God. We feel after His will and His ways. I'm amazed at all the people who seem to always know everything God is saying about everything. My faith looks for Him because my eyes can't always see. On the other hand, there is a healthy reaction that occurs in blindness; our senses become keener as we exercise what we don't normally need. God knows what it will take to bring us to a place of searching. He knows how to stir us from our tranquil and comfortable perching position of supremacy. There are times when even our great sages of this age murmur in the night. Behind the scenes we tremble in our hearts at the presence of God,ZO whose sovereign will often escapes the realm of our human reasoning.

🌸 Matthew 7:7 tells me to "Seek and you will find"—so I will continue to seek His will and pathway for my life when I…

When told to seek God, I am somewhat confused because I feel His presence so often within me and surrounding me—as a normal part of my life. What does this mean?

Talking Foolishness

Then Job replied to the Lord: "I know that you can do anything, and no one can stop you. You asked, 'Who is this that questions my wisdom with such ignorance?' It is I—and I was talking about things I knew nothing about, things far too wonderful for me" (Job 42:1-3 NLT).

I believe there are times when we grow weary of human answers. The crucial times that arise in our lives require more than good advice. We need a word from God. There are moments when we need total seclusion. We come home from work, turn off the phone, close the blinds, and lie before God for a closer connection. In Job's case, he was going through an absolute crisis. His finances were obliterated. His cattle, donkeys, and oxen were destroyed. His crops were gone. In those days it would be comparable to the crash of the stock market. It was as if Job, the richest man, had gone bankrupt. What a shock to his system to realize that all are vulnerable. It is sobering to realize that one incident, or a sequence of events, can radically alter our lifestyles.

🌿 Am I working from paycheck to paycheck? Is my savings account large enough to carry me over a financial crisis?

❧ Do I question God's wisdom? And am I "big" enough to answer God the way Job did when facing disaster?

Stop Brooding

Then Job answered the Lord and said: "I know that You can do everything, And that no purpose of Yours can be withheld from You. You asked, 'Who is this who hides counsel without knowledge?' Therefore I have uttered what I did not understand, Things too wonderful for me, which I did not know" (Job 42:1-3 NKJV).

Through his financial devastation, Job probably could have reached out to his children for comfort, but they were gone too. His marriage had deteriorated. Then he also became ill. Have you ever gone through a time in your life when you felt you had been jinxed? Everything that could go wrong, did! Frustration turns into alienation. Maybe that time is now. So now what? Will you use this moment to seek God or to brood over your misfortune? With the right answer, you could turn the jail into a church! In your hardest season, you have two choices. You can turn toward God or turn away. You can become desperate and seek God or become bitter and blame God. Beloved, stretch out your hands to reach after Him. Don't let bitterness overtake you. Cry out to God for His wisdom and blessing.

🌿 When faced with financial and/or family crises, I usually:

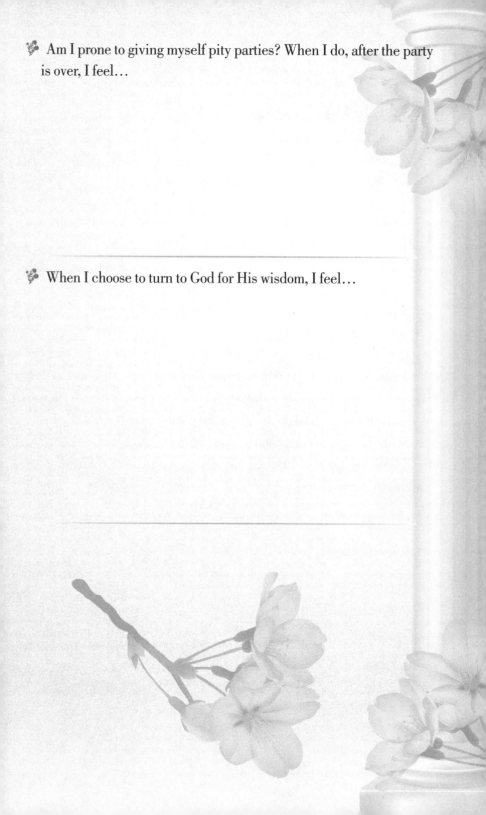

🌸 Am I prone to giving myself pity parties? When I do, after the party is over, I feel…

🌸 When I choose to turn to God for His wisdom, I feel…

Evil's Trick

> *Look, I go forward, but He is not there, and backward,*
> *but I cannot perceive Him; when He works on the left*
> *hand, I cannot behold Him; when He turns to the right*
> *hand, I cannot see Him* (Job 23:8-9 NKJV).

Comfort comes when you know that the present adversity will soon be over. But what comfort can be found when it seems the problem will never cease? Read the Scripture passage above again. This is Job speaking. It is terrifying when you see no change coming in the future. Job was saying, "I see no help, no sign of God, in the future." This is actually satan's trick to make you think help is not coming. That hopelessness then produces anxiety. Like a rainstorm that will not cease, the waters of discouragement begin to fill the tossing ship with water. Suddenly you experience a sinking feeling. However, there is no way to sink a ship when you do not allow the waters from the outside to get inside! If the storms keep coming, the lightning continues to flash, and the thunder thumps on through the night, what matters is keeping the waters out. Keep that negative thinking out of your spirit!

🌾 I too often allow negative thoughts to rule over my:

During times of troubles when I feel the waters of discouragement trying to seep into my mind, I will…

No Stupor Sitting

> *But if I go to the east, he is not there; if I go to the west,*
> *I do not find him. When he is at work in the north, I*
> *do not see him; when he turns to the south, I catch no*
> *glimpse of him* (Job 23:8-9 NIV).

Like a desperate sailor trying to plug a leaking ship, Job frantically cast back and forth in his mind, looking for some shred, some fragment of hope, to plug his leaking ship. Exasperated, he sullenly sat in the stupor of his condition and sadly confessed that he catches no glimpse of God. "I can't find Him where I thought He would be." Have you ever told yourself that the storm would be over soon? And the sun came and the sun left, and still the same rains beat vehemently against the ship. It almost feels as if God missed His appointment. You thought He would move by now! Glancing nervously at your watch you wonder, *Where is He?!* Remember, dear friend, God doesn't synchronize His clock by your little mortal watch. He has a set time to bless you; just hold on.

🌿 When I think my boat is about to sink, I will read Matthew 8:24-26 and rest knowing that Jesus is in the boat with me and…

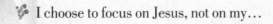

🌿 I choose to focus on Jesus, not on my…

Gross Insanity

The Lord replied, "I will personally go with you, Moses, and I will give you rest—everything will be fine for you" (Exodus 33:14 NLT).

Quite honestly, there are moments when life feels like it has all the purpose of gross insanity. Like a small child cutting paper on the floor, there seems to be no real plan, only actions. These are the times that try men's hearts. These are the times when we seek answers. Sometimes, even more than change, we need answers. "God, if You don't fix it, please, please explain it!" We are reasoning, resourceful creatures. We seek answers. Yet there are times that even after thorough evaluation, we cannot find our way out of the maze of happenstance! Where is the God who sent an earthquake into the valley of dry bones and put them together (see Ezekiel 37)? The truth is, our God is never far away. The issue is not His presence as it is our perception. Many times deliverance doesn't cost God one action. Deliverance comes when our minds accept His timing and purpose in our lives.

❦ God promises to go with me and that He will give me rest—He assures me that everything will be fine for me. So then why do I…

I don't doubt God's love or promises, but…

His Presence Is the Answer

Then he said to me, "Speak a prophetic message to these bones and say, 'Dry bones, listen to the word of the Lord! This is what the Sovereign Lord says: Look! I am going to put breath into you and make you live again!'" (Ezekiel 37:4-5 NLT).

In my hours of crises, many times I found myself searching for the place of rest rather than for the answer. If I can find God, I don't need to find money. If I can find God, I don't need to find healing! If I can find Him, my needs become insignificant when I wave them in the light of His presence. What is a problem if God is there? Even in the stench of Job's decaying flesh, he knew that his answer wasn't screaming out for the healing. He was screaming out for the Healer! Do you realize the power of God's presence? I hear many people speak about the acts of God, but have you ever considered the mere presence of God? He doesn't have to do anything but be there, and it is over!

🌿 If I can find God, I don't need to find…

🌿 When I realize the power of God's presence, I have…

Searching Through Rubbish

> *Then Job spoke again: "My complaint today is still a bitter one, and I try hard not to groan aloud. If only I knew where to find God, I would go to his court. I would lay out my case and present my arguments"* (Job 23:1-4 NLT).

No wonder Job was sitting in sackcloth and ashes searching through the rubbish of his life, looking for God. He knew that only the presence of the Lord could bring comfort to his pain! Have you begun your search for a closer manifestation of His grace? Your search alone is worship. When you seek Him, it suggests that you value Him and recognize His ability. The staggering, faulty steps of a seeker are far better than the stance of the complacent. He is not far away. He is in the furnace, moving in the ashes. Look closer. He is never far from the seeker who is on a quest to be in His presence. God is not far away, my friend. If you don't know what He's doing in your life right now, if everything feels confusing, just rest in His presence—and keep searching.

🌸 Confusion turns to clarity when I accept God's timing and purpose, which I will do by:

🌿 Would I rather search through the rubbish in my life for God or search through His Scriptures full of wisdom and truth?

On the Other Hand

And He said to me, "My grace is sufficient for you, for My strength is made perfect in weakness." Therefore most gladly I will rather boast in my infirmities, that the power of Christ may rest upon me (2 Corinthians 12:9 NKJV).

Have you been searching and seeking and yet feel that you are getting no closer? Perhaps you are closer than you think. Job told us where to find God. He told us where He works. Job said that God works on the left hand! I know you've been looking on the right hand, and I can understand why. The right hand in the Bible symbolizes power and authority. That's why Christ is seated on the right side of God (see Mark 16:19). Whenever you say someone is your "right hand," you mean that person is next in command or authority. Naturally, then, if you were to search for God, you would look on the right hand. Granted, He is on the right hand. He is full of authority. But you forgot something. His strength is made perfect in weakness (see 2 Corinthians 12:9). He displays His glory in the ashes of human frailty. He works on the left hand!

❦ Yes, of course God is ambidextrous. To me this revelation means that He can…

I will list my weaknesses here and then write beside each one how God has used each one for His glory and my benefit.

Strength from Weakness

Each time he said, "My grace is all you need. My power works best in weakness." So now I am glad to boast about my weaknesses, so that the power of Christ can work through me (2 Corinthians 12:9 NLT).

Great growth doesn't come into your life through mountaintop experiences. Great growth comes through the valleys and low places where you feel limited and vulnerable. The time God is really moving in your life may seem to be the lowest moment you have ever experienced. Most believers think that God works when the blessing comes. That's not true! God is working on you, your faith and your character, when the blessing is delayed. The blessing is the reward that comes after you learn obedience through the things you suffered while waiting for it! I wouldn't take any amount of money for the things I learned about God while I was suffering. Between every step of faith, between every new dimension of exaltation, there will always be some level of struggle. If there is no valley, there is no mountain.

🌺 What I like most about the mountaintop experiences:

🌺 What I like most about valley experiences:

Be Strong and Courageous

> *So be strong and courageous! Do not be afraid and do not panic before them. For the Lord your God will personally go ahead of you. He will neither fail you nor abandon you* (Deuteronomy 31:6 NLT).

There is another issue to discuss about living on the left side of God. It is difficult to perceive God's workings on the left hand. God makes definite moves on the right hand, but when He works on the left, you may think He has forgotten you. If you've been living on the left side, you've been through a period that didn't seem to have the slightest stirring. It seemed as if everything you wanted to see God move upon stayed still. "Has He gone on vacation? Has He forgotten His promise?" you've asked. The answer is no! God hasn't forgotten. You simply need to understand that sometimes He moves openly. I call them right-hand blessings. But sometimes He moves silently, tiptoeing around in the invisible, working in the shadows. You can't see Him, for He is working on the left side! How long does God work on the left? I don't know. But I do know that God has never taken His eye off you— He knows where you are every minute.

🌺 Oh, what a comfort it is to know that God is…

🦋 I will take time to seriously seek God's face in the shadows and listen for His stealth footsteps in my life where He is…

With Either Hand

The heavens declare the glory of God; the skies proclaim the work of his hands (Psalm 19:1 NIV).

I know so well how hard it is to trust Him when you can't trace Him! But that's exactly what He wants you to do—He wants you to trust Him with either hand. It may seem that everybody is passing you right now. Avoid measuring yourself against other people. God knows when the time is right. His methods may seem crude and His teachings laborious, but His results will be simply breathtaking. Without scams and games, without trickery or politics, God will accomplish a supernatural miracle because you trusted Him while He worked on the left side. If you feel God is working on the left side in your life, spend time in prayer today committing to trust Him again. Pour out your heart, cry out for help, but commit to hold on. He has never forsaken you, so don't you forsake Him!

❧ Sometimes I wonder where I am spiritually—where I stand with God, my heavenly Father; I pray He sees me as…

❧ I know God won't abandon me and that His Holy Spirit lives within me, but…

As Pure as Gold

He knows where I am going. And when he tests me, I will come out as pure as gold (Job 23:10 NLT).

Now you sit on the Master's right side, ready and available to be used, a vessel of honor unto Him. No matter how glorious it is to sit on His right hand and be brought to a position of power, just remember that although you have overcome now, you were boiled down and hollowed out while you lived on the left side of God. I'm happy also because God tested me, not my enemies. Not the devil, but God! I wouldn't trust anybody else but Him to take me through these left-side experiences. He loves me enough to give me everything I need to live with Him on the left side. Look back over your left-side experiences for a brief time. Taste the bitter tears and the cold winds of human indifference. It's our secret, whether we tell them or sit quietly and make small talk. You've not always been where you are or shined as you shine. What can I say? You've come a long way, baby!

🌿 I'm so proud of myself for…

🌿 I thank God because He…

Small Beginnings

> *Do not despise these small beginnings, for the Lord rejoices to see the work begin…* (Zechariah 4:10 NLT).

I remember so well the early struggles that my wife and I had to maintain our family, finances, and overall well-being while building a ministry. I was working a secular job that God wanted me to leave for full-time ministry. I was scarcely asked to preach anywhere that offered more than a few cakes, jars of jelly, and maybe enough gas money to get home. I learned to preach in tiny churches around old coal stoves. Finally I said yes to full-time ministry because the company I worked for went out of business. What a frightening experience to find myself without a job and then a car and then utilities and often without food. I scraped around doing odd jobs to feed two children and a wife. But I am proud to tell you that I experienced God in those desperate days of struggle. God is not in a rush with you. He has all the time in the world. If you're still in your small beginning, trust that you're right where He wants you. Don't try to rush this season.

🌿 My small beginnings in my faith journey started with:

🌿 I'm proud to write that during my faith journey, I:

The Liar

So Satan answered the Lord and said, "Does Job fear God for nothing? Have You not made a hedge around him, around his household, and around all that he has on every side? You have blessed the work of his hands, and his possessions have increased in the land. But now, stretch out Your hand and touch all that he has, and he will surely curse You to Your face!" (Job 1:9-11 NKJV)

Satan cannot dispute your serving God, but he challenges our reason for serving Him. He says it is for the prominence and protection that God provides. He further insinuates that if things weren't going so well, we would not praise God so fervently. The devil is a liar! In one way or another, we will face times when we must answer satan's charges and prove that even in the storm, He is still God! My early years of challenge were hard. My pride, my self-esteem, and my self-confidence teetered like a child learning to ride a bicycle. My greatest fear was that it would never end. I feared that, like someone stuck in an elevator, I would spend the rest of my life between floors—neither here nor there in a permanent stage of transition. I learned, however, to remember my beginnings while reaching toward my goals. Then God blessed me and I had no fear that my accomplishments would become idols in my life. The same is true for you.

🌸 My greatest fear is that…

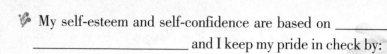 My self-esteem and self-confidence are based on _____
_____ and I keep my pride in check by:

Grace to Endure

God saved you by his grace when you believed. And you can't take credit for this; it is a gift from God (Ephesians 2:8 NLT).

Often we don't realize how severe our beginnings were until we are out or about to come out of them. When you are in those small beginnings, it can feel like it will never end. That was my biggest fear. The concern over the future coupled with the fear of failure bring us to the posture of prayer. I don't think I completely realized how severe my early years were because I saw them through the tinted glasses of grace. I had been gifted with the grace to endure. What a gift to look back and see He never once left my side. What a gift to be purified in God's fire and endure. I can't say it enough: God has a purpose for your life. He will bless you…in His time. Have you accepted the grace to endure, beloved? Ask God to show you His perspective on your small beginnings, whether they are in the past or the present.

🌿 I haven't always understood what grace really means. Today I will search the Scriptures and ask the Holy Spirit to…

The grace to endure specifically brings to mind this one particular incident that…

Time to Grow

For unto us a Child is born, unto us a Son is given; and the government will be upon His shoulder. And His name will be called Wonderful, Counselor, Mighty God, Everlasting Father, Prince of Peace (Isaiah 9:6 NKJV).

When the first man Adam was created, he was created full grown. He had no childhood, no small beginning. He was immediately a man. But the last man Adam—Jesus—was born a child. The Bible says He grew in favor with God and all the people (see Luke 2:52). Once I was praying for the Lord to move mightily in my ministry. I had asked, fasted, prayed, and probably begged a little, but none of it hurried the plan of God in my life. After many days of absolute silence, God finally answered by saying, "You are concerned about building a ministry, but I am concerned about building a man." He concluded with this warning, which has echoed in my ears all of my life. He said, "Woe unto the man whose ministry becomes bigger than he is!" Since then I have prayed for the minister, not for the ministry. I am still amazed at who I am becoming as I put my life daily into His hands. He is changing me. Every day I see more immaturity in me. But what a sharp contrast I am now to what I was. Please allow yourself to grow.

❧ I admit that I want to be "mature" in my faith, career, relationships—now! I will change my daily prayer to asking God to build...

 Patience is something I need to…

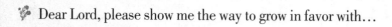 Dear Lord, please show me the way to grow in favor with…

Have Peace

These things I have spoken to you, that in Me you may have peace. In the world you will have tribulation; but be of good cheer, I have overcome the world (John 16:33 NKJV).

What a joy it is to be at peace with who you are and where you are in your life. How restful it is to not try and beat the clock with friends or try to prove anything to foes. You will never change their minds anyway, so change your own. I want to be better—to have a better character, better confidence, and a better attitude! The desire to be bigger allows no time to rest, relax, or enjoy your blessing. The desire to be better, however, affords you a barefoot stroll down a deserted beach to sit on the sand, throw shells into the water, and shiver when the tide rushes up too high. You can sing into the wind a song out of tune that is full of therapy. There are probably many things you didn't get done and so much you have left to do. But isn't it nice you have the time and freedom to sigh, relax, and just thank God for the things—the little, tiny, small challenges—that you know He brought you through. Thank God for small things.

🌸 I'm thankful for:

I want to be better at:

No-Discount Promises

> *If what has been built survives, the builder will receive a reward* (1 Corinthians 3:14 NIV).

Many people want to be successful, but not everyone realizes that success is given only at the end of great struggle. If it were easy, anybody could do it. Success is the reward that God gives to the diligent who, through perseverance, obtain the promise. When I was a youngster, we kids used to change the price tags on the items we could not afford. We weren't stealing, we thought, because we did pay something, just not the real price. Many people try to do the same thing today in their spiritual life. They want a discount on the promises of God. That doesn't work in the Kingdom. Whatever it costs, it costs; there's no swapping the price tags. You must pay your own way. Your payment helps you to appreciate the blessings when they come because you know the expense. You will not easily jeopardize the welfare of something not easily attained. The zeal it takes to be effective at accomplishing a goal ushers you up the steps of life.

🌿 In my work life I work hard to be successful; in my spiritual life I work hard to…

🌿 I'm willing to pay the price to move forward in my faith journey by:

Desires

> *Delight yourself also in the Lord, and He shall give you the desires of your heart* (Psalm 37:4 NKJV).

Successful people tend to be passionate people who have intense desire. I admit there are many passionate people who are not successful. But if you can focus your passion for a divine purpose, you will be successful. Some people never use their desire in a positive way. Instead of harnessing it and allowing it to become the force they use to overcome hindrances, it becomes a source of frustration and cynicism. Success only comes to a person who is committed to a cause or has a passion to achieve. It takes more than a mere whimsical musing over a speculative end. It takes floor-walking, devil-stomping, anointed tenacity to overcome the limitations that are always surrounding what you want to do for your God, yourself, and your family!

🌿 Today the desires of my heart include:

🌿 Thinking about my passions and desires leads me to feeling…

Cain's Children

Then the Lord said to Cain, "Why are you angry? Why is your face downcast? If you do what is right, will you not be accepted? But if you do not do what is right, sin is crouching at your door; it desires to have you, but you must rule over it" (Genesis 4:6-7 NIV).

It is amazing the relationships that can be lost as you travel upward. As you journey up the steps to purpose, promise, and blessing, it becomes increasingly difficult to be successful without others finding you offensive. Some people will find your success offensive, whether or not you are arrogant. They are offended at what God does for you. I call those people "Cain's children." They will murder you because you have God's favor. Watch out for them. They will not rejoice with you. They can't be glad for you because somehow they feel your success came at their expense. They foolishly believe that you have their blessing. No diplomacy can calm a jealous heart. They don't want to pay what you paid, but they want to have what you have. Cain's children will invite you into their field to destroy you.

❧ How many of these people are in my life and I haven't noticed?

❧ I will be on the lookout for any of Cain's children who mean to harm me by…

Defense Mode

Your enemies will be right in your own household!
(Matthew 10:36 NLT).

How can you defend yourself from another person's reaction to you? Being defensive can make you become imprisoned by paranoia. It is difficult to be careful without being distrustful and cynical. "Are we not brothers and sisters?" Sure we are. Yet Jesus said that our enemies will be right in our own household. Your enemy will not wound you if you are too far away. To be a good Judas, he or she must be at the table with the victim of his betrayal! Who sits at your table? Imagine Jesus, at the height of His ministerial career, sitting at the table with John, the beloved, on one side, and Judas, the betrayer, on the other. The problem is discerning which is which. Both are intimate, but one is lethal. You must depend on the Lord and keep your affections on the Giver, not the gifts. "Lord, help us to keep our eyes on the things that will not change."

🌿 I don't like to think that I have enemies; I'm not one for confrontations, yet I realize that there is evil in the world. Therefore I must…

🌿 Always being focused on the Giver of promises and blessings will keep me…

Fear Not

So you must remain faithful to what you have been taught from the beginning. If you do, you will remain in fellowship with the Son and with the Father (1 John 2:24 NLT).

As long as you're in the day of small beginnings, you're acceptable. People don't always want to see you move on—especially if they perceive you as moving more rapidly than they are. Or receiving more favor and blessing. As painful as it is to be criticized by those you are in covenant with, it's far worse to give up the course that God has for you just for their acceptance. As you need to be affirmed and understood, at some point you must ask yourself, "How much am I willing to lose in order to be accepted?" Don't let this scare you or make you defensive. Instead, keep your eyes fixed on God and fellowship with this true friends, like John was to Jesus. If you are facing criticism and ridicule, don't let it get you off course. Surrender negative comments and unjust judgments back to God—and forgive those who have not celebrated you.

🌺 Criticism—good and bad—is hard to hear and accept. I pray that the Lord will clearly reveal what I should accept and what I should reject. In this way I can be assured of…

🕊 I also pray that God will allow only friends like John into my life—
and He will help me identify any like Judas so I may…

The Cost of Blessings

The master said, "Well done, my good and faithful servant. You have been faithful in handling this small amount, so now I will give you many more responsibilities. Let's celebrate together!" (Matthew 25:23 NLT).

With every blessing there is an additional responsibility. How many times have you prayed for a blessing? Then when you received it, you realized there were strings attached that you didn't originally consider? To be honest, being blessed is hard work. Everything God gives you requires maintenance. God gave Adam and Eve the Garden, but they still had to tend it. There is a "down" side to every blessing. Jesus said that no one starts building without counting the cost (see Luke 14:28-30). You must ask yourself if you are willing to pay the price to get the blessing. Just with these questions alone, we have weeded out all the women who say they want a husband and children but don't want to cook, care, or clean. We have also weeded out all the men who say they want a wife but don't want to love, provide, and nourish! Most people are in love with the image of success but haven't contemplated the reality of possessing the blessing.

🌿 How willing am I to pay the price of the blessing I have been praying for?

Have I counted the cost of this blessing? What added responsibilities will come with this blessing?

Immune Deficiency

We have endured no end of ridicule from the arrogant,
of contempt from the proud (Psalm 123:4 NIV).

If you are always weeping over rejection and misunderstanding, if you're always upset over who doesn't accept you into their circles anymore, you may be suffering from an immune deficiency syndrome. You waste precious time of communion when you ask God to change the minds of people. It is not the people or the pressure that must change; it is you. In order to survive the stresses of success, you must build up an immunity to those things that won't change. Thank God that He provides elasticity for us. If you really want to pursue your dream, there is a place in God where you build up an immunity to the adversity of success. It is simply a matter of survival. Remember, you can't switch price tags just because you don't like the price. There must be an inner growth in your ability to withstand the struggles that accompany the things you have. My constant prayer is, "Lord, change me until this doesn't hurt anymore."

🌿 I admit that it does hurt when someone ridicules me, but I will pray for that person and...

Today I will look to the Lord for confirmation and affirmation rather than to someone who…

Great Excitement

Zacchaeus quickly climbed down and took Jesus to his house in great excitement and joy (Luke 19:6 NLT).

I love to surround myself with people who can stir up the fire in me. Some people in the Body of Christ know just what to say to ignite the very fire in you. However, no one can ignite in you what you do not possess! If the cold winds of opposition have banked the fire and your dream is dying down, I challenge you to rekindle your desire to achieve whatever God has called you to do. Don't lose your fire. You need that continued spark for excellence to overcome all the blight of being ostracized. Fire manifests itself in two ways. First, it gives light. Whenever you maintain your fire, it produces the light of optimism against the blackness of crises and critics alike. As long as you maintain that fire-like attitude, you will find a way to survive the struggle. A person never dies with a twinkle in his eyes. Second, fire gives heat. Heat can't be seen, but it can be felt. When you are burning with the passion to survive, the heat can be felt. Invisible but effective, your intensity is always detected in your speech and attitude.

🌿 How "fired up" am I about inviting Jesus into my life, home, workplace, and relationships?

How much spiritual heat do people feel when I am near them? Are they warmed by God's presence? Do they see His light shining through me?

Feed the Fire

For this reason I remind you to fan into flame the gift of God, which is in you through the laying on of my hands (2 Timothy 1:6 NIV).

Every man and woman of God must remember that fire needs fuel. Feed the fire. Feed it with the words of people who motivate you. Feed it with vision and purpose. When stress comes, fan the flames. Gather the wood. Pour gasoline on it if you have to, but don't let it die! How many cold nights I have warmed my cold feet by the fires of my innermost desire to complete a goal for my life. No one knows how hot the embers glow beneath the ashes of adversity. Is your fire blazing or has it died down to embers? Ask the Holy Spirit to show you how to fan the flames. Especially ask Him to highlight other people in your life who can stir up the fire. Focus on those friendships as you press on toward your goals.

🌿 Family and friends who know how to fan the flame of God's gift in me include:

🌿 Foes who try and extinguish the godly flame in my life include:

🌸 May I always know the difference between the two by:

Ask for Your Blessing

> *Just as a body, though one, has many parts, but all its many parts form one body, so it is with Christ* (1 Corinthians 12:12 NIV).

Sometimes just seeing God bless someone else gives you the fortitude to put a demand on the promise that God has given you. I don't mean envy, but a strong provocation to receive. I have learned how to rejoice over the blessings of my brother and realize that the same God who blessed him can bless me also. If seeing others blessed makes you want to sabotage their success, then you will not be fruitful. Other people's blessings ought to challenge you to see that it can be done. Don't begrudge other people's blessings; simply ask for your own. Your assignment is to dig for your own gold. Success cannot be defined in generalities; it can be defined only according to individual purpose and divine direction. Cultivate what the Lord has given to you.

🌿 I try hard not to compare myself to other people, but it's not easy sometimes when…

🌿 I am successful in the following areas of life:

More Is Required

…When someone has been given much, much will be required in return; and when someone has been entrusted with much, even more will be required (Luke 12:48 NLT).

Not everyone can handle success. Some may choose tranquility over notoriety. They don't like criticism and they abhor pressure. But if you are the kind of person who desperately needs to attain the hope of your calling, then go for it. Some people will never be satisfied with sitting on the bench cheering for others who paid the price to play the game. Locked within them is an inner ambitious intrigue not predicated on jealousy or intimidation. It is built upon an inner need to unlock a predestined purpose. For them, it does not matter. Inflationary times may escalate the price of their dreams, but whatever the price, they are compelled, drawn, and almost driven toward hope of attainment.

Success to me means:

At times, the price of my dreams coming true is:

Live Without Regret

...let us run with perseverance the race marked out for us (Hebrews 12:1 NIV).

I am not afraid of dying as much as I am afraid of not living first. What absolutely terrifies me is the thought that I stand beside life like a miser who longs for a certain article but is too crippled by incessant fear of expense to buy. If you want it, pay the price. I confess, I have cried huge salty tears. I have felt the bitter pangs of rejection and criticism. I admit there were times when I rocked my worries to sleep in the middle of the night. Know all this and understand that I have not yet seen a day that made me regret the decision to run my course. How far or how fast you run in comparison with others doesn't matter. What matters is that you stretch your legs and run. You run only against your own shadow. You stride beside your own destiny. Don't let fear stop you. Don't let other people push you down. Run your race as the powerful person of God you really are. Live without regret.

🌺 Am I more afraid of dying or of not fully living?

🌺 To live without regret means...

Run with Endurance

Therefore we also, since we are surrounded by so great a cloud of witnesses, let us lay aside every weight, and the sin which so easily ensnares us, and let us run with endurance the race that is set before us (Hebrews 12:1 NKJV).

I am told that distance runners make long, steady strides with emphasis on endurance, not speed. They take their laps and stretch their limitations, committing their strength to a goal. Turning corners with agility, running shoes banging the pavement, heads high, backs straight—they are in pursuit of a goal. I am told that as they near the finish line, there is a final burst of energy that kicks in like the final cylinders in an engine. It is the last lap; no excuses; it's now or never. Now they go for broke! At least once, before they roll you in on a slab and put a name tag on your cold, stiff toe, you owe it to your God and to yourself to experience in some area in your life that last-lap feeling of giving your all. I want to warn you, though; it hurts to push yourself. It's not easy to get up early every morning while others sleep and prepare for the challenge. Like Jesus in the garden of Gethsemane, it is difficult to find someone who will stand with you while you are in preparation. But there can be no celebration without preparation.

🌿 The weight and sin ensnaring me and keeping me from giving my all are a combination of:

I will prepare for my long-distance race, and especially that last lap, by:

Stand

May the God who gives endurance and encouragement give you the same attitude of mind toward each other that Christ Jesus had (Romans 15:5 NIV).

The question is universal but the answer is totally individual. Can you stand to be blessed? If you answer yes, then the only way to be blessed is to stand! When you can't seem to put one foot in front of the other, stand. When days come that challenge your destiny, just stand. Realize that there has never been a day that lasted forever. You can't afford to crumple onto your knees like a weak, whimpering lily blown over by a windstorm. You can't stand the pain of a cross unless there is something more important than the pain you endure in the process. Your purpose is worth any cost. Don't stop short of the finish line. Give all that is in you to run your course. Remember, you are not running alone. A great cloud of witnesses is cheering you on (see Hebrews 12:1). Look to Jesus. Build the endurance of faith and the muscles of perseverance so you will also get the gold.

❧ Standing firm on my convictions has always been:

❧ The endurance of my faith and the muscles of my perseverance were tested in my life when:

Ready, Set, Win

> *Don't you realize that in a race everyone runs, but only one person gets the prize? So run to win!* (1 Corinthians 9:24 NLT).

A s you're running your race on this earth, there must be something beyond the acquisition of a goal. Many people spend all their lives trying to attain a goal. When they finally achieve it, they still secretly feel empty and unfulfilled. This will happen even in the pursuit of godly goals and successes if we don't reach beyond the mere accomplishment of an ambitious pursuit. In short, success doesn't save! Why then does God put the desire to attain in the hearts of His men and women if He knows that at the end is only, as Solomon so aptly put it, "Vanity of vanities...all is vanity" (Ecclesiastes 12:8 NKJV)? In other words, as another translation states, "Meaningless! Meaningless!...Everything is meaningless!" (NIV). It could be that we who have achieved something of effectiveness must then reach a turn in the road and begin to worship God beyond the goal!

🌾 Have I ever reached a goal and my elation was short-lived?

When racing toward achieving a goal, God must be my focus because only He…

Eternal Prize

We pleaded with you, encouraged you, and urged you to live your lives in a way that God would consider worthy. For he called you to share in his Kingdom and glory (1 Thessalonians 2:12 NLT).

There is a prize beyond the finish line. When we build in this world, there is actually an eternal Kingdom work being done in our lives. God is with us and for us, and as we achieve our unique purpose, His eternal Kingdom comes. If we build in our own strength for our own glory, there is no divine purpose. That's when we feel like Solomon, empty at the end. Even the greatest achievements won't satisfy you without God's presence. But when you see God holding a giant trophy, standing at the end of your race, you can't help but praise Him. He created us to achieve and to build, but it must be unto His glory and for His purpose in our lives.

🌸 What am I yearning to achieve today?

🌸 Is there an eternal purpose behind my efforts to accomplish this achievement?

Here Am I

Also I heard the voice of the Lord, saying: "Whom shall I send, and who will go for Us?" Then I said, "Here am I! Send me" (Isaiah 6:8 NKJV).

Why are we always such extremists? Some of us spend all our lives doing absolutely nothing for the Lord. We are constantly in His presence, praising His name, but we fail to accomplish anything relative to His purpose. As an eagle stirs her nest, so God must challenge us to leave the familiar places and perform the uncertain future of putting into practice the total of all we have learned in the Lord's presence. God's presence is the cocoon where we receive identity and purpose. Full joy and abundant life are in Him. What makes us think we can do the work of the Lord and never spend time with the Lord of the work? As Isaiah said, "Here am I! Send me" (Isaiah 6:8). Choose to be a vessel God can use!

🌿 How easy would it be for me to respond as Isaiah did?

🌿 When was the last time I did something significant to advance the Kingdom of God?

Only God Satisfies

*Everyone who competes in the games goes into strict
training. They do it to get a crown that will not last,
but we do it to get a crown that will last forever* (1 Corinthians 9:25 NIV).

After we reach a goal, we do not continue to celebrate what we have already accomplished. The beauty of the moment soon fades; there must be something beyond just achieving goals and setting new goals. You would be surprised at the number of pastors and leaders who race wildly from one goal to the other without ever feeling fulfilled by their accomplishments. It is the cruelest form of torture to be secretly dying of the success that others envy. You need to strive, but you don't need the obsession that it can create. There will never be anything that God gives you to do that will replace what God's mere presence will give. You will never build your self-esteem by accomplishing goals, because once you've done it, it's done! Only Christ can save you, affirm you, and speak to how you feel about yourself.

✤ There have been times when all my striving left me feeling…

✤ Reaching goals or accomplishments may boost my self-esteem for the short term, but continually focusing on God will…

Hello, God Calling

> *…the twenty-four elders fall down before Him who sits on the throne and worship Him who lives forever and ever, and cast their crowns before the throne, saying: "You are worthy, O Lord, To receive glory and honor and power; for You created all things, and by Your will they exist and were created"* (Revelation 4:10-11 NKJV).

We as Christians reach fulfillment when we bring to the Lord all that we have and worship Him on the other side of accomplishment. This need to return an answer to the Sender is as instinctive as answering a ringing phone. There is a ringing in the heart of a believer that requires an answer. We answer a ringing phone because of our insatiable curiosity to know who is calling. God is calling us. His ring has sounded through our triumphs and conquests. A deep sound in the recesses of a heart turned toward God suggests that there is a deeper relationship on the other side of the blessing. As wonderful as it is to be blessed with promises, there is still a faint ringing that suggests the Blesser is better than the blessing. Many people overlook the ring. The bustling, blaring sound of survival can be deafening. There must be a degree of spirituality to hear and respond to the inner ringing of the call of God! Like the 24 elders in Revelation, you must learn to trade a monument for a moment. The real reward you need to seek can be paid only by God Himself.

🌿 For me, on the other side of accomplishment is…

I will never miss the chance to answer God's call because He…

Humble Beginnings

So humble yourselves under the mighty power of God, and at the right time he will lift you up in honor (1 Peter 5:6 NLT).

I have a question for you. What makes a connoisseur of fine restaurants leave the elegant, aristocratic atmospheres and the succulent cuisine of gourmet food, only to stop by a hamburger joint for a sandwich and fries? Time's up. Here's the answer. Each of us has within us a need for balance and a sense of normalcy. It is so important that we balance our areas of expertise with plain everyday humanism. I started out preaching in the most adverse of circumstances. I went from sleeping in a child's bedroom in somebody's home to penthouse suites. I remember ministering in churches where the finances did not allow for a hotel room or even a real guest room. This evangelist would stay with the pastor, and usually the pastor had a house full of children. One of these bright-eyed children would have to give up his or her room to accommodate this man of God. I still pray for those families who gave what they had to make me as comfortable as they could. I earnestly appreciate it.

🌿 Being humble:

_____ comes naturally to me.

_____ is something I can do if I think about it.

_____ is hard for me.

🌿 The last time I chose to be humble in a situation was when…

The Lord's Prayer

In this manner, therefore, pray: Our Father in heaven, hallowed be Your name. Your kingdom come. Your will be done on earth as it is in heaven. Give us this day our daily bread. And forgive us our debts, as we forgive our debtors. And do not lead us into temptation, but deliver us from the evil one. For Yours is the kingdom and the power and the glory forever. Amen (Matthew 6:9-13 NKJV).

The disciples asked the Lord to teach them how to pray. When Jesus taught on prayer, He was teaching us how to steer the ship of life through the boisterous winds of adversity. If we can follow the "manner" of prayer, then we can follow the course of life. In order to pray effectively, we must know the personage of God. Hence He said, "Our Father." This establishes the basis of the relationship that we have with God. He is more than just Creator. He is our Father. We must know that we are related to God and not just created by Him. "[I]n heaven" addresses the fact that the God I am related to is the Ruler of the universe. The Bible teaches us that Heaven is God's throne. So when we say, "Our Father in heaven," we are proclaiming God's absolute sovereignty. This phrase points directly to God's position. Now knowing the Person and the position of Him, let us praise Him in prayer.

🌿 How often do I repeat this prayer without really thinking about each word and phrase?

How amazing that Jesus Himself taught His disciples—and me—how to pray to Father God. From this day forward I will…

In This Manner

> *In this manner, therefore, pray: Our Father in heaven, hallowed be Your name. Your kingdom come. Your will be done on earth as it is in heaven. Give us this day our daily bread. And forgive us our debts, as we forgive our debtors. And do not lead us into temptation, but deliver us from the evil one. For Yours is the kingdom and the power and the glory forever. Amen* (Matthew 6:9-13 NKJV).

Dear Father God, "I am not ashamed to praise You as I know the extent of Your authority. I take this time to approach You correctly. 'Hallowed be Your name.' I almost forgot that just because You are my Father, my 'Abba,' that doesn't give me the right to show disrespect for Your position as Ruler in Heaven and earth. So 'hallowed be Your name' reminds me that I must enter into Your gates with thanksgiving and into Your courts with praise" (see Psalm 100:4). Praise will turn God's head. It gets His attention. I dare you to learn how to praise His name. When you praise His name, you are praising His character. He is "above board." He is holy!

🌿 The dictionary defines the word "hallowed" as:

🌿 To me in the context of this prayer, the word "hallowed" means…

From Power to Purpose

In this manner, therefore, pray: Our Father in heaven, hallowed be Your name. Your kingdom come. Your will be done on earth as it is in heaven. Give us this day our daily bread. And forgive us our debts, as we forgive our debtors. And do not lead us into temptation, but deliver us from the evil one. For Yours is the kingdom and the power and the glory forever. Amen (Matthew 6:9-13 NKJV).

The first verse in the Lord's Prayer is about who God is and lifting His name with praise. When praises go up, blessings come down. So here comes the downpour of power. "Your kingdom come" releases the downpour of the power of God. Praise will cause the very power of God to come down in your life. But what good is power without purpose? Thus Jesus taught the disciples, "Your will be done on earth, as it is in heaven." That is a step up from power to purpose. Now the purpose of God comes down to your life. You can't have success without purpose! "Give us this day our daily bread" deals with the provisions of Heaven coming down. This is more than a prayer; it is a divine direction. After receiving the power in your life, you come to understand the purpose. When you know your purpose, God will release the provisions.

Today I pray that God releases a downpour of His power on me to…

🌺 I gladly accept God's provisions from Heaven so I may…

Key Connection

In this manner, therefore, pray: Our Father in heaven, hallowed be Your name. Your kingdom come. Your will be done on earth as it is in heaven. Give us this day our daily bread. And forgive us our debts, as we forgive our debtors. And do not lead us into temptation, but deliver us from the evil one. For Yours is the kingdom and the power and the glory forever. Amen (Matthew 6:9-13 NKJV).

Now Jesus teaches His disciples to pray for a forgiving heart. "Forgive us our debts, as we forgive our debtors." Repentance is also flowing down from the throne. Finally, Jesus taught us to seek deliverance from evil. Pray for the problems that still exist at every stage, and better still, at every success in life! If you were raised in church, you probably prayed this prayer hundreds of times. Sometimes something becomes so familiar that we forget the meaning of the words behind it. I've taken apart the prayer Jesus taught His disciples so you can really understand how to pray, know what each word is communicating. Jesus didn't even start His ministry until the Father spoke over Him. Then He constantly broke free from the crowd to pray, to communicate with His Father, being constantly connected to God. Let this prayer go deep into your heart. Every word and phrase is a key to connection with your Father. Reality check:

🌿 I am:

_____ quick to forgive.

_____ quick to condemn.

I want God to:

_____ quickly forgive me.

_____ quickly condemn me.

The Turning Point

And in this manner, therefore, pray: Our Father in heaven, hallowed be Your name. Your kingdom come. Your will be done on earth as it is in heaven. Give us this day our daily bread. And forgive us our debts, as we forgive our debtors. And do not lead us into temptation, but deliver us from the evil one. For Yours is the kingdom and the power and the glory forever. Amen (Matthew 6:9-13 NKJV).

Having briefly examined the progression of the believer through this precious prayer that Jesus taught His disciples, let us move on to the real point: the turning point. God wants you to receive all of the great successes and accolades that He promised in His Word, but having received them, you must go beyond them to enter a level of understanding. None of this success is as important or as valuable as you initially thought. At this stage of life you reevaluate what you call success. God gets the glory when you turn from all He gave you and say from your heart, "Lord, I've found nothing as dear to me as You. My greatest treasure is the assurance of Your divine presence on my life. I am giving it all to You. 'For Yours is the kingdom,'—yes, I know I just prayed it down, but here it is. I am giving it back to You. Wait a minute, Lord. I want to say something else. 'And the power.' You can have that too. Oh, and about all that glory I've been getting—it's Yours as well! How long? Forever and ever and ever. It is so! Amen!"

🌱 Yes! I want to go beyond any success I attain to acknowledge that God...

God, Yours is the…

Re-Gifting

O God, we give glory to you all day long and con-stantly praise your name (Psalm 44:8 NLT).

Every aspect of creation that receives anything gives it back to God. The gold cornfields of the Midwest give back seed after the heavens send down the rains. The busy bee fills the air with the testimony of the pollen taken from the lilac and rose and gives back in the sweetness of the honey in the comb. The mineral kingdom gives strength to the vegetable kingdom. Everything reaches the point of return. An apple tree eventually needs to give apples back to the ground it grew from. In every person's life comes a turning point. If you fail to recognize and praise God, all your achievements will quickly lose their luster. There is no real joy outside of fellowship with your Creator. We are created to receive and to give back heartfelt praises.

🌿 I'm choosing to re-gift the blessings God has showered me with by…

🌿 My most prized achievement gives God the glory when I…

Every Good and Perfect Gift

> *Whatever is good and perfect is a gift coming down to us from God our Father, who created all the lights in the heavens. He never changes or casts a shifting shadow* (James 1:17 NLT).

Ten men were healed, but to the one who returned Jesus added the privilege of being whol. (see Luke 17:11-19). Many will climb the corporate ladder. Some will claim the accolades of this world. But soon all will realize that success, even with all its glamour, cannot heal a parched soul that needs the refreshment of peace. Nothing can bring wholeness like the presence of God. Perhaps you are the one in ten who has the discernment to know that the blessing is nothing without the One who caused it to happen. Most people are so concerned about their immediate needs that they fail to take the powerful experience that comes from a continued relationship with God! Remember, healing can be found anywhere, but wholeness is achieved only when you return to the Healer with all of your heart and thank Him for the miracle and the gift of a second chance.

🌿 May I always remember to thank God for His good and perfect gifts, including His…

Although I am not a leper as in Luke 17, the Healer gifted me when He…

A Time to...

To everything there is a season, a time for every purpose under heaven: A time to be born, and a time to die; a time to plant, and a time to pluck what is planted; a time to kill, and a time to heal; a time to break down, and a time to build up; a time to weep, and a time to laugh; a time to mourn, and a time to dance (Ecclesiastes 3:1-4 NKJV).

Do you remember how in winter icicles hang from the roofs of old houses, pointing toward the ground like stalactites in a cave? As the cold blitz of winter was challenged by budding trees and warmer days, the icicles dripped and diminished. Slowly the earth changed its clothes for a new season. As a child, I can plainly remember the joys of each season. We packed away our sleds as spring came. We traded coats for sweaters, then discarded them for shirt sleeves as the sun liberated us from our wintry cocoons. In twilight silence, the sap hidden in the bottom of the trees moved upward like a sluggish elevator making its ascent to the top. In the morning light, buds turned to blossoms and by summer the blossoms showed their fruit. It is good to prepare for each season, but don't demand fruit out of season. Ask God to teach you His rhythm so you can move in sync with Him. Don't worry, you'll bear your fruit in the right time.

🌿 My favorite season in my physical life is when...

My favorite season in my spiritual life is when…

God's Almanac

Yet I am confident I will see the Lord's goodness while I am here in the land of the living. Wait patiently for the Lord. Be brave and courageous. Yes, wait patiently for the Lord (Psalm 27:13-14 NLT).

Presuming that you now understand the necessity of small beginnings, and presuming that you realize whatever you have will not replace the One who gave it and that success only creates a platform for responsibility to be enlarged—then you can begin to ascertain where you are on the calendar, the divine almanac of God. Did you know that God has an almanac? Perhaps you do not know what an almanac is. My mother always consulted the almanac to determine the best time to plant the crop she intended to harvest. It is a calendar that presents the seasons and cycles of a year. You see, the principle of seed time and harvest will not override the understanding of time and purpose. God does everything according to His eternal almanac of time and purpose!

🌿 The timing for most of my life activities usually goes according to plan because I…

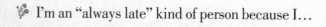

🌿 I'm an "always late" kind of person because I…

Wise Counsel and Prayer

> *Then Esther sent this reply to Mordecai: "Go and gather together all the Jews of Susa and fast for me. Do not eat or drink for three days, night or day. My maids and I will do the same…"* (Esther 4:15-16 NLT).

Esther was a wise woman. Once Mordecai had provided wise counsel, she called a time of fasting and prayer to prepare her spirit. She knew that prayer undergirds the spirit and keeps a person from sagging beneath the weight of opposition. Not only did she pray, but she also taught everyone under her authority to pray as well. I have learned that it is difficult to work with people who do not pray. Even our children pray. Now I'm not suggesting that we are perfect. We don't pray because we are perfect—we pray because we are not! Prayer is a strong defense against satanic attack. If Esther had not prayed, she would have fallen prey to the cunning devices of Haman, her wicked enemy! Counsel may prepare your mind, but only fervent prayer can prepare your spirit for the vast undertakings that come with it being your time in God's plan, purpose, and blessing.

🌿 My thoughts about fasting include:

🌿 Prayer and fasting lead to:

Timing Is Everything

If you keep quiet at a time like this, deliverance and relief for the Jews will arise from some other place, but you and your relatives will die. Who knows if perhaps you were made queen for just such a time as this?" (Esther 4:14 NLT).

If you want to be part of God's great purposes on the earth, I admonish you to be someone who engages routinely in fervent prayer. Esther was chosen by God for a significant mandate. God positioned her in a place of authority with great influence. She had the ear of the king, who had the power to save her people. If you want to be elevated to a position of influence, make sure you search your heart and motivations. If somewhere deep down you're still looking for the affirmation of people, it won't go well for you. Esther did not take her position lightly. She knew she could only succeed in her mission if God backed her up, so she ardently sought Him. Beloved, you also have the ear of the King. He has placed you on the earth for such a time as this! Don't miss your time.

🌿 In my prayers today, I will whisper in the ear of my King…

🌿 I don't want to miss my time to make a difference in my world and God's Kingdom by…

Songs of Joy

Those who sow with tears will reap with songs of joy. Those who go out weeping, carrying seed to sow, will return with songs of joy, carrying sheaves with them (Psalm 126:5-6 NIV).

The most frightening thing I can think of is the possibility of missing my time. Generally, somewhere on the other side of a tremendous test is the harvest of your dream. If you have planted the seeds of a promise and watered them thoroughly with the tears of struggle, then this is your time. Woe to the person who has seeds without water. The tears of struggle become the irrigation of the Holy Spirit. Through your tear-filled struggles God directs the waters of life to the field of your dreams. On the other hand, don't overwater the promise! A certain amount of tears is necessary, but when you have come to harvest, don't let the devil keep you weeping. Joy is for the harvester. Reap with joy. You've paid your dues and shed your tears—now reap your benefits. It's your turn!

🌿 How comforting it is to know that after sowing good seeds with tears I will be reaping a good harvest with joy. I look forward to…

The Bible tells me in Psalm 56:8 (NLT) that "You keep track of all my sorrows. You have collected all my tears in your bottle. You have recorded each one in your book." This is proof that...

The Prepared Believer

Put on your armor, and take up your shield. Prepare for battle, and come to my aid (Psalm 35:2 NLT).

This is an exciting time for the prepared believer. I believe many are coming into "green light" times. You feel as though you have been waiting without seeing any results, almost like a car waiting at an intersection. Then the light suddenly changes from red to green and you are free to move. When God changes the light in your life from red to green, you can accomplish what you couldn't before. How exciting to suddenly find your engine kicking into gear and you're on the road again. I believe with all my heart that people will burst to the fore-front and pull into the fast lane. Trained by patience and humbled by personal challenges, they will bring a new season into the Kingdom. Are you part of what God is doing? I want to see you burn some spiritual rubber for Jesus! As a prepared believer you are actively ready for what God wants to do in your life. Get ready, the light's about to change!

🌿 Am I a prepared believer? Yes, because I…

🌿 How fast can I respond to moving forward when the red light changes to green?

No Holding Back

For the Lord God is our sun and our shield. He gives us grace and glory. The Lord will withhold no good thing from those who do what is right (Psalm 84:11 NLT).

There may be some degree of reservation in the mind of the thinking person: "What if I enter my season and experience the rich blessings God has been promising for a long time, and then the season ends? Isn't it difficult to become subdued and lethargic after being exposed to the racing, titillating feeling of a 'green light' time in life?" First, let me rebuke the spirit of fear. Declare God's victory over your fear. Also, we must not fall in love with what God is doing—we must always be in love with who God is. People have a need to know what comes next. God doesn't always make us privy to such information, but He has promised that if we walk uprightly, He will not withhold any good thing from us (see Psalm 84:11). So I conclude that if God ends a season, it was no longer working for my good. And I'm ready for the next assignment, which will be good for me.

🌿 Knowing that God gives me grace and glory and all good things makes me…

🌿 Doing what is right comes easier the longer I…

Peace to Enjoy Life

Preach the word; be prepared in season and out of season; correct, rebuke and encourage—with great patience and careful instruction (2 Timothy 4:2 NIV).

When I was a young man, there was an elderly lady in our church who used to sing a song that went something like, "Anyway You bless me, Lord, I'll be satisfied." What a wonderful place to be—where you can trust the God whom you have believed upon to operate for your ultimate good. There is a peace that Christians must have to enjoy life. There always is an area where you can be fruitful—it simply may not be the same area each time. We must always remember that God can bless us even during the waiting periods of our lives. There are really no "down" times in God. We only feel down when, like spoiled children, we demand that He continue to give us what He did at one stage without appreciating the fact that we are moving to another stage. Romans 1:17 (NKJV) calls it going from faith to faith. God has trained you to be productive in a variety of areas.

🌿 I'm satisfied with my life whenever…

🌿 I seek to have peace during each stage and season of life, appreciating the special…

Set Free

> *A woman was there who had been crippled by a spirit for eighteen years. She was bent over and could not straighten up at all. When Jesus saw her, he called her forward and said to her, "Woman, you are set free from your infirmity"* (Luke 13:11-12 NIV).

The Holy Spirit periodically lets us catch a glimpse of the personal testimony of one of the patients of the Divine Physician Himself. This woman's dilemma is her own, but perhaps you will find some point of relativity between her case history and your own. She could be like someone you know or have known; she could even be like you. There are three major characters in this story—the person, the problem, and the prescription. It is important to remember that for every problem, our God has a prescription! Although the problem may be rooted in the past, the prescription is a present word from God! The Word is the same yesterday, today, and forevermore (see Hebrews 13:8)! That is to say, the word you are hearing today is able to heal your yesterday!

🌱 Being set free from any problem, including physical issues, is one of the greatest blessings to accept. I do so willingly so that…

🌱 I call on the Divine Physician Himself to bless me with…

Good Judgment

Teach me knowledge and good judgment, for I trust your commands (Psalm 119:66 NIV).

One of the greatest struggles I have encountered is the temptation to make permanent decisions based on temporary circumstances. Someone once said, "Patience is a tree whose root is bitter, but its fruit is sweet." The reward of patience is reflected in gradually not having to amend your amendments. Temporary circumstances do not always require action. I have found that prayer brings us into patience. Patience results from trust. We cannot trust a God we don't talk with. Do not misunderstand me; God needs men and women who are decisive. However, every situation shouldn't get an immediate reaction. Prayer is the seasoning of good judgment. Without it, our decisions will not be palatable.

🌱 I admit that I rush to judgment, not always good judgment. I will correct this hasty reaction by:

🌱 Today I will trust that the bitter root of patience will produce sweet fruit, which I will use to make:

God Is Love

For God so loved the world that He gave His only begotten Son, that whoever believes in Him should not perish but have everlasting life (John 3:16 NKJV).

Healing cannot come to a desperate person rummaging through other people's lives. Hurting people need to break the habit of using others as a narcotic to numb the dull aching of an inner void. The more they medicate the symptoms, the less chance of allowing God to heal and bless. Another destructive tendency is to keep increasing the dosage. We must avoid addictive, obsessive relationships. If you are becoming increasingly dependent upon anything other than God to create a sense of wholeness in your life, you are abusing your relationships. Clinging to people is far different from loving them. It is not so much a statement of your love for them as it is a crying out of your need for them. Like lust, it is intensely selfish. It is taking and not giving. Love is giving. God is love. God proved His love not by His need of us but by His giving to us His Son, Jesus.

🌿 I have been (or am currently) in an abusive relationship and…

🌿 Abuse of any kind prevents God's love from being fully embraced; therefore…

Blessing the Brokenhearted

The Spirit of the Lord is upon Me, because He has anointed Me to preach the gospel to the poor; He has sent Me to heal the brokenhearted, to proclaim liberty to the captives and recovery of sight to the blind, to set at liberty those who are oppressed (Luke 4:18 NKJV).

Approximately five out of ten marriages end in divorce. Those broken homes leave a trail of broken dreams, people, and children. Only the Master can heal these victims in the times in which we live. He can treat the long-term effects of this tragedy. One of the great healing balms of the Holy Spirit is forgiveness. To forgive is to break the link between you and your past. Sadly enough, many times the person hardest to forgive is the one in the mirror. Although they rage loudly about others, people secretly blame themselves for a failed relationship. Regardless of who you hold responsible, there is no healing in blame! When you begin to realize that your past does not necessarily dictate the outcome of your future, then you can release the hurt. I pray that God would give the grace of releasing so you can receive the blessings God has for you now. Exhale, then inhale; there is more for you.

🌿 I have been brokenhearted and it was _____ to forgive the person who hurt me because...

🌸 Right now, Lord God, please give me the grace to release everyone I am still blaming for my...

Unity

Now all of us can come to the Father through the same Holy Spirit because of what Christ has done for us. So now you Gentiles are no longer strangers and foreigners. You are citizens along with all of God's holy people. You are members of God's family (Ephesians 2:18-19 NLT).

There is a devilish prejudice in the Church that denies the blood of Christ to its uncomely members. The spirit of Cain is loose in the Church! We have spilled our brother's blood because they are different, because her skin or his sin is different from ours. Untie them right now, in the name of the Lord, and restore to them the opportunity to experience the life that only comes to the flesh through the blood. Without the blood all flesh dies—black, white, rich, poor, homosexual, heterosexual, drug addict, or alcoholic. Without the blood of Christ to save and the Holy Spirit to empower, no flesh can be saved—no blessing received.

🌿 Sometimes I feel uncomfortable when in church and someone sits beside me who...

🌿 How open are my arms to welcome people who are different from the way I act, think, worship?

Only God

> *Only I can tell you the future before it even happens. Everything I plan will come to pass, for I do whatever I wish. I will call a swift bird of prey from the east—a leader from a distant land to come and do my bidding. I have said what I would do, and I will do it* (Isaiah 46:10-11 NLT).

I can remember as a very small child following close behind my mother, an educator in the public school system. She was often asked to speak at luncheons and banquets. We were traveling from one of these events when I said to my mother, "Today, I travel with you and listen while you speak, but the time will come when you will travel with me and I will speak!" This prophetic utterance came from the mouth of a then-devilish little six-year-old who, though very precocious, was nevertheless an ordinary child who would one day have a supernatural encounter with God! I knew even then that I had an appointment with destiny—I sensed that God had a purpose for my life. I earnestly believe that everyone is predestined to accomplish certain things for the Lord. Somewhere in the recesses of your mind there is an inner knowing that directs you toward an expected end.

✤ This recollection intrigues me because…

Having an "appointment with destiny" stirs my heart in a way that…

Prophetically Speaking

…What I have said, that I will bring about; what I have planned, that I will do (Isaiah 46:11 NIV).

I don't think I really knew I would be a minister. I just felt that I would do something meaningful with my life. Twice in my childhood I spoke prophetically about things that have since come to pass. I can't say that everything I encountered in life pushed me toward my destiny. On the contrary, there were sharp contradictions as I went through my tempestuous teens. Still, I had that inner knowing, too deep to be explained. I want you to know that even if circumstances contradict purpose, purpose will always prevail! It is the opposition that clearly demonstrates to you that God is working. If the fulfillment of the prophecy was without obstruction, you would assume you had merely received serendipity. However, when all indicators say it is impossible and it still occurs, then you know God has done it again.

At times it seemed as if someone was speaking prophetically over me when…

When reading God's Word, I have sometimes felt as if…

Grace and Truth

> *Yet God, in his grace, freely makes us right in his sight. He did this through Christ Jesus when he freed us from the penalty for our sins* (Romans 3:24 NLT).

The glory of God is manifested only when there is a balance between grace and truth. Religion doesn't transform. Legalism doesn't transform. God doesn't have to punish you to bless and heal you. Jesus has already prayed for you. Believe the Word of God and be free. Jesus our Lord was a great emancipator of the oppressed. It does not matter whether someone has been oppressed socially, sexually, or racially—our Lord is an eliminator of distinctions. God has no favorites. He tears down barriers that would promote prejudice and separation in the Body of Christ. I understand that morality is important in Christianity; however, there is a great deal of difference between morality and legalism. God is balanced, not an extremist.

🌾 Religion and legalism in a church bring division and…

🌾 Sincere and true Christianity bring _____to the Church and to the world.

While Still Sinners

But God showed his great love for us by sending Christ to die for us while we were still sinners (Romans 5:8 NLT).

I can't help but wonder what would happen if we would love like Jesus loves. As we peel away layer by layer, as we become more comfortable with our God and our own humanity, we become increasingly transparent. Perhaps we can learn how to be as open about our failures as we are about our successes. Without that kind of honesty, we create a false image that causes others to needlessly struggle. When others hear our one-sided testimony of successes with no failure, they become discouraged. They feel as if they don't qualify to receive what God has done for us because we have falsified the records and failed to tell the truth. When you find someone who can see your flaws and your under-developed character, and love you in spite of it all, you are blessed!

❧ Loving like Jesus loves means that I would want to…

❧ If I create a false image around others, it's usually because I…

Holding Pattern

But those who wait on the Lord shall renew their strength; they shall mount up with wings like eagles, they shall run and not be weary, they shall walk and not faint (Isaiah 40:31 NKJV).

While traveling on a major American airline, we were told that the plane could not land at its scheduled time. Evidently the air traffic controller instructed that we should wait in the air. What a strange place to have to wait—in the air! I have often felt like that aircraft suspended in the air when God says, "Wait!" Then the captain spoke, saying, "We are going to assume a holding pattern until further instructions come from the tower." After some time, a few rather intoxicated passengers began to question the traffic controller's decision. The flight attendant calmly and quickly eased people's fears, informing us that planes always carry enough fuel to withstand delays. I began to wonder if we as the children of God shouldn't be better prepared for those times in our lives when God speaks from His throne, "Assume a holding pattern until further notice." Then the question becomes: "Do you have enough faith to assume a holding pattern and wait for the fulfillment of the promise?"

🌿 After being told to wait, is my response anything close to how some of those airline passengers reacted?

🌺 Do I have enough faith to assume a holding pattern and wait for the fulfillment of God's promise and blessing?

God's Goodness

> *Or do you despise the riches of His goodness, forbear-*
> *ance, and longsuffering, not knowing that the goodness*
> *of God leads you to repentance?* (Romans 2:4 NKJV).

It sounds mushy, and to the religious zealot it may sound too loose and simplistic, but we need to remember that it is the goodness of God that leads to repentance. Repentance doesn't come because of the scare tactics and threats of raging ministers who need mercy themselves. Repentance comes because of the unfailing love of our perfect God, the God who cares for the cracked vases that others would have discarded. His great love causes a decision to be made in the heart: I must live for Him! He will stand with you when all others forsake you—you will want to please Him! There is no way you can weather a storm in His loving arms and not say, "I am Yours, O Lord. What I have I give to You." One gaze into His holiness brings sinners crashing to the floor on bended knees, confessing and forsaking, wrestling and controlling every issue that would have engulfed them before they beheld the manifold graces of God!

🌿 May I never despise the riches of God's goodness and patience when He is dealing with my…

May I be found open and honest and repentant with God about my sins so He will…

By His Blood

> *Therefore, my beloved, as you have always obeyed, not as in my presence only, but now much more in my absence, work out your own salvation with fear and trembling; for it is God who works in you both to will and to do for His good pleasure* (Philippians 2:12-13 NKJV).

We have no right to be blessed, in ourselves. We are neither worthy nor deserving of it. Yet He has blessed us "in spite of us." Our testimony must change. Away with the polished brass words from silver-spooned lips that suggest anonymity from failure and fear. There is a great deal of difference between the cold callousness of a rebellious heart and the deeply troubled heart of a transforming Christian whose whispered prayer is, "God, save me from myself." It is to the distraught heart that seeks so desperately for a place of refuge that we extend soft hands and tender words. The precious blood of Christ brought us here. Beneath the streaming tears of a grateful heart, through our trembling lips must emerge the truth that Christ has done it all, and that we have nothing to boast in but His precious blood—His blood alone!

🌿 I have often/sometimes/never whispered, "God, save me from myself" in response to…

🦋 I confess that I am not worthy or deserving of God's grace or mercy, *but* because of the blood of Christ, I accept all that God…

Death on a Cross

Instead, he gave up his divine privileges; he took the humble position of a slave and was born as a human being. When he appeared in human form, he humbled himself in obedience to God and died a criminal's death on a cross (Philippians 2:7-8 NLT).

To fully understand the precious effect of Jesus' blood, we must take a look back at Calvary's bloody banks. As the eclipsed sun tucked itself behind the trembling ground, a ground still wet with the cascading blood of a loving Savior, Jesus' love was so awesome that it could only be depicted by the morbidity of His dying. Allow this country preacher, this West Virginia hillbilly, a final glimpse at the only hope his soul has of Heaven. Brush a tear from a face full of thanksgiving and look at His bruised, mutilated, and lacerated body. Look at the 33-year-old body that was filled with such youth and potential, which now hangs from the cross. From His beaten back to His ripped torso, we see a wounded knight without armor. His garments lie crumbled on the ground, the object of the desires of His villainous guards who now gamble up their leisure moments, waiting on the death angel to flap his wings in the face of the Savior.

🌿 It's hard to even think about the agony my Savior endured for me, so I more than often don't…

Oh, how many times have I turned away from the gruesome details of His final hours, just too painful to...

Still Preaching

*He personally carried our sins in his body on the cross
so that we can be dead to sin and live for what is right.
By his wounds you are healed* (1 Peter 2:24 NLT).

The Savior's head is pricked with the thorns of every issue that would ever rest on my mind. His hands are nailed through for every vile thing I have ever used mine to do. His feet are nailed to the tree for every illicit, immoral place you and I have ever walked in! Sweat and blood race down His tortured frame. His oozing, gaping wounds are tormented by the abrasive bark of that old rugged cross and are assaulted by the salty sweat of a dying Man. In spite of His pain and abuse, in spite of His torment and His nudity, He was still preaching as they watched Him dying—naked and not ashamed!

🌿 Only God's Son could absorb all of humanity's sins into His physical body so all of humanity could have the opportunity to accept His offer of eternal life. This reality is…

🌿 Jesus gave His life for me. I give my life to Him as a…

Spiritual Arrogance

> But the Scriptures declare that we are all prisoners
> of sin, so we receive God's promise of freedom only by
> believing in Jesus Christ (Galatians 3:22 NLT).

Jesus condemned the Pharisees for their spiritual arrogance, yet many times that self-righteous spirit creeps into the Church. There are those who define holiness as what someone wears or what a person eats. For years churches displayed the name "holiness" because they monitored a person's outward appearance. They weren't truly looking at character. Often they were carried away with whether someone should wear makeup or jewelry, when thousands of people were destroying themselves on drugs and prostitution. Priorities were confused. Unchurched people who came to church had no idea why the minister would emphasize outward apparel when people were bleeding inside. All humans were born in sin, equally and individually shaped in iniquity, and not one race or sociological group has escaped our sinful heritage.

🌿 I pray, Lord, that You will expose any spiritual arrogance in me so I can…

🌿 Do I place more emphasis on a person's appearance than on the condition of their soul and heart?

Get Up Again

The godly may trip seven times, but they will get up again. But one disaster is enough to overthrow the wicked (Proverbs 24:16 NLT).

Sometimes Christians give up on life because of personal struggles. They think it's all over, but God says not so! The best is yet to come. The Lord doesn't like pity parties, and those who have them are shocked to find that although He is invited, He seldom attends. Many morbid mourners will come to sit with you as you weep over your dear departed dreams. But if you want the Lord to come, don't tell Him you aren't planning to get up. The whole theme of Christianity is of rising again—and you can't rise until you fall. That doesn't mean you should fall into sin. It means you should allow the resurrecting power of the Holy Spirit to operate in your life. It doesn't matter what tripped you—it matters that you rise up. I would rather walk on the water with Jesus and nearly drown than to play it safe and never experience the miraculous.

🌾 I will rise as many times as I have to in accordance with God's…

🌾 Pity parties are no longer part of my social life—rather, my parties will be…

Accepted Unconditionally

> *God decided in advance to adopt us into his own family by bringing us to himself through Jesus Christ. This is what he wanted to do, and it gave him great pleasure. So we praise God for the glorious grace he has poured out on us who belong to his dear Son* (Ephesians 1:5-6 NLT).

In my early days as a new Christian, I tried to become what I thought all the other Christians were. Secretly suffering from low self-esteem, I thought that the Christians around me had mastered a level of holiness that seemed to evade me. I deeply admired those virtuous "faith heroes" whose flowery testimonies loftily hung around the ceiling like steam gathering above a shower. They seemed so changed, so sure, and so stable! I admired their standards and their purity, and earnestly prayed, "Make me better, Lord!" I don't think I have changed that prayer, but I have changed the motivation behind it. I began to realize that in God's perfect love, He knew me and loved me as I was. All I had known was love based on performance. If I did well today, God loved me. However, if I failed, He did not love me. What a roller-coaster ride! I didn't know from moment to moment whether I was accepted in the beloved or not!

🌱 Do I strive to be like others in church who seem to be more spiritual than I am?

❦ Have I accepted the fact that God's love for me is perfect and unconditional, not based on performance?

Your New Self

You were taught, with regard to your former way of life, to put off your old self, which is being corrupted by its deceitful desires; to be made new in the attitude of your minds; and to put on the new self, created to be like God in true righteousness and holiness (Ephesians 4:22-24 NIV).

Why did God bring this miraculous new creature so easily into the lives of some people when it seemed so far removed from others (like me)? I didn't realize that the "new self" starts out as a child who has to grow into the mature character and nature of the Lord. No one shared with me that they had experienced struggles before they obtained victories. It is important to let God mature us—without our self-help efforts to impress others with a false sense of piety. That kind of do-it-yourself righteousness and religion keeps us from being naked before God and from being comfortable with our own level of growth. Yes, I want to be all that God wants me to be. But while I am developing at the rate He has chosen, I will certainly thank Him for His rich grace and bountiful mercy along the way. This is the divine mercy that lets us mature naturally.

🌸 I know I have put my old self behind me when I think about how I…

Sometimes I am too much of a self-help Christian thinking I can…

The Church Is a Hospital

He heals the brokenhearted and binds up their wounds
(Psalm 147:3 NIV).

People must be loosed from the chains of guilt and condemnation. Many women in particular have been bound by manipulative messages that specialize in control and dominance. The Church must open its doors and allow people who have a past to enter in. What often happens is that they spend years in the back pew trying to pay through deference for something in the past. The Bible never camouflaged the weaknesses of the people God used. God used David. God used Abraham. We must divorce our embarrassment about wounded people. Yes, we have wounded and hurting people. Sometimes they break the boundaries and they become lascivious and out of control and we have to readmit them into the hospital and allow them to be treated again. That's what the Church is designed to do. The Church is a hospital for wounded souls.

🌿 I was/am hurt and I desperately sought/am seeking godly solace and direction from fellowship in the Body of Christ, reaching out to…

🌿 I was/am wounded by someone in a church and was/am still unsure about attending church ever again, yet in my spirit I…

Be Relentless

Not only so, but we also glory in our sufferings, because we know that suffering produces perseverance; perseverance, character; and character, hope (Romans 5:3-4 NIV).

"Relentless" is a word I use to describe people who will not take no for an answer. They try things one way, and if that doesn't work, they try it another way. Don't give up. You may feel as if you are about to break beneath the stress of intense struggles—don't quit! A terrible thing happens to people who give up too easily. It is called regret. It is the nagging, gnawing feeling that says, "If I had tried harder, I could have succeeded." It is terrible to lie down at night thinking, *I wonder what would have happened if I had tried this or that.* Granted, we all experience some degree of failure. That is how we learn and grow. The problem isn't failure; it is when our lack of commitment forfeits an opportunity to turn the test into a triumph! We can never be sure of the answer unless we rally our talents, muster our courage, and focus our strength to achieve a goal. We must have the passion to be relentless.

🌿 I don't consider myself a quitter, but…

🌿 During intense struggles I tend to…

Jars of Clay

But we have this treasure in jars of clay to show that this all-surpassing power is from God and not from us (2 Corinthians 4:7 NIV).

While we are changed in our spirit by the new birth, our old corruptible body and fleshly desires are not. They are Spirit-controlled, but not Spirit-destroyed! The Holy Spirit is living with us in a stinking clay pot—a putrid, decaying, clay-covered, vile body. Its stench is so bad that we must continually wash and perfume it just to endure living there ourselves. Yet God Himself, the epitome of purity, has forsaken the rich, robust pavilions of His holy domain to live in a failing, decaying, deteriorating, collapsing, and corroding shell.

🌿 I ask myself many times why God would choose to live in me. My answer always comes back to:

🌿 I will follow Jesus' teaching when He tells me in Matthew 26:41 and Mark 14:38, "Watch and pray so that you will not fall into temptation. The spirit is willing, but the flesh is weak." That way I can rest assured that I…

God's Dwelling Place

In him the whole building is joined together and rises to become a holy temple in the Lord. And in him you too are being built together to become a dwelling in which God lives by his Spirit (Ephesians 2:21-22 NIV).

Within our decaying shells, we constantly peel away, by faith, the lusts and jealousies that adorn the walls of our hearts. If the angels were to stroll through the earth with the Creator and ask, "Which house is Yours?" He would pass by all the mansions and cathedrals, all the temples and castles. Unashamedly, He would point at you and me and say, "That house is Mine!" Imagine the shock and disdain of the heavenly host to think that the God whose face they fan with their wings would choose to live in such a shack and shanty! We know where our greatest conflict lies. We who blunder and stumble in our humanity, we who stagger through our frail existence—we continually wrestle with the knowledge that our God has put so much in so little!

❧ It's true, I do wrestle knowing that God chose to dwell in me—I'm only worthy of that honor because…

❧ Knowing God lives in me makes me want to clean out every dark corner where I keep my…

This Old House

> *I have been crucified with Christ; it is no longer I who live, but Christ lives in me; and the life which I now live in the flesh I live by faith in the Son of God, who loved me and gave Himself for me* (Galatians 2:20 NKJV).

Despite all our washing and painting, all our grooming and exercising, this old house is still falling apart! We train it and teach it. We buy books and tapes, and we desperately try to convince it to at least think differently. But like a squeaky hinge on a swollen door, the results of our efforts, at best, come slowly. There is no doubt that we have been saved, and there is no doubt that the house is haunted. The Holy Spirit Himself resides beneath this sagging roof. Although the tenant is prestigious, the accommodations are still substandard.

🌿 How haunted is this house of mine where the Lord of the universe chose to live?

🌿 Lord God, I know that my efforts to clean out Your dwelling place are fruitless unless I depend on the Holy Spirit, which I will do today. And with His help…

God's Divine Occupation

> *But the officer said, "Lord, I am not worthy to have you come into my home…"* (Matthew 8:8 NLT).

God's divine occupation is not an act of a desperate guest who, having no place else to stay, chose this impoverished site as a temporary place to ride out the storm of some deplorable situation. No, God Himself has—of His own free will and predetermined purpose—put us in the embarrassing situation of entertaining a Guest whose lofty stature so far exceeds us that we hardly know how to serve Him!

🌸 Only because of Jesus, my Savior, can God even step over the threshold of His dwelling place in me. That is why…

🌸 God chose to live in me because…

Rodents and Roaches

For we know that if the earthly tent we live in is destroyed, we have a building from God, an eternal house in heaven, not built by human hands. Meanwhile we groan…Now the one who has fashioned us for this very purpose is God, who has given us the Spirit as a deposit, guaranteeing what is to come (2 Corinthians 5:1-2,5 NIV).

So the bad news is that the old house is still a death trap; it's still infested with rodents. A legion of thoughts and pesky memories crawl around in our heads like roaches that come out in the night and boldly parade around the house. Add to this pestilence an occasional groaning in the dungeon, and you have a view of the inner workings of a Christian! That should not negate our joy, though; it merely confesses our struggles. We have not been taught about the crying of the Spirit, but I tell you that the Holy Spirit can be grieved. He has the capacity and ability to groan within us until His groaning emerges as conviction in the heart of the humble. Yes, it is bad news, but the Guest we entertain desires more for us than what we have in us! He enjoys neither the house nor the clothing we offer Him. He just suffers it like a lover suffers adversity to be in the company of the loved one.

When I read the passage from 2 Corinthians 5, my spirit…

I've heard and felt a groan in my spirit when I…

A House Divided

Jesus knew their thoughts and said to them, "Every kingdom divided against itself will be ruined, and every city or household divided against itself will not stand" (Matthew 12:25 NIV).

The good news is that the bad news won't last long! Jesus says that every city or house divided against itself shall not stand. Ever since we were saved, there has been a division in the house. Eventually the old house will have to yield to the new one! Yes, we are constantly renovating through the Word of God, but the truth is that God will eventually recycle what you and I have been trying to renovate! Only then will the groaning of the regenerated spirit within us transform into sheer glory!

🌿 Oh, how I look forward to that sheer glory, because then I know…

🌿 Until then, I will constantly renovate through reading and absorbing all that God has to tell me in His holy Scriptures—starting with the book of _____.

A Sacrificial Life

I discipline my body like an athlete, training it to do what it should. Otherwise, I fear that after preaching to others I myself might be disqualified (1 Corinthians 9:27 NLT).

The very best of us camouflage the very worst in us with religious colloquialisms that reduce Christianity to more of an act than an attitude. Even the most pious among us—while in the quiet booth of some confessional or kneeling in solitude at the edge of our beds—must murmur our confession before God: "We earnestly pursue a place in You that we have not yet attained." Our struggle feeds the ravenous appetite of our holy Guest, whose divine hunger requires us to perpetually feed Him a sacrificial life. He daily consumes, and continually requires, what we alone know God wants from us. The apostle Paul battled to bring into submission the hidden things in his life that could bring destruction. Whatever they were, he declared war. He says, in essence, that as he waits for the change, he disciplines his body, beating back the forces of evil.

🌿 Daily I will, like Paul, discipline my body so that…

🌿 Daily I will also feed God the fruits of my obedience as I…

The Rescuer

> *For he* [God] *has rescued us from the dominion of darkness and brought us into the kingdom of the Son he loves* (Colossians 1:13 NIV).

Many people who were part of the ministry of Jesus' earthly life had "colorful" pasts. A good example is Matthew, who was a tax collector. Few people like tax collectors still today. Tax collectors back then did more than receive taxes for the benefit of the government. They were frequently little better than common extortioners. Regardless of his past, Jesus called Matthew to be a disciple, a great apostle, and he wrote one of the books of the New Testament. Much of the history and greatness of Jesus would be lost if not for Matthew. We must maintain a strong line of demarcation between a person's past and present. Jesus was criticized for being around the oppressed and the rejected. They followed Him—knowing He offered mercy and forgiveness.

🌿 I have been in need of being rescued when…

🌿 With the help of the Holy Spirit, I will "rescue" people by sharing the gospel—starting with…

Tailored Efforts

Soldiers don't get tied up in the affairs of civilian life, for then they cannot please the officer who enlisted them. And athletes cannot win the prize unless they follow the rules (2 Timothy 2:4-5 NLT).

Whenever we bring our efforts into alignment with His purpose, we automatically are blessed. In order to win the prize, our efforts must be tailored after the pattern of divine purpose. Everyone is already blessed. We often spend hours in prayer trying to convince God that He should bless what we are trying to accomplish. What we need to do is spend hours in prayer for God to reveal His purpose. When we do what God has ordained to be done, we are blessed because God's plan is already blessed. I learned that God will not be manipulated. If He said it, that settles it. No amount of praying through parched lips and tear-stained eyes will cause God to avert what He knows is best for you.

🌿 I'm definitely a rule follower type of person, but sometimes I doubt…

🌿 Sometimes I'm not sure what God has ordained to be done, which keeps me from…

Internal Conflict

> *For in my inner being I delight in God's law; but I see another law at work in me, waging war against the law of my mind and making me a prisoner of the law of sin at work within me. What a wretched man I am! Who will rescue me from this body that is subject to death?* (Romans 7:22-24 NIV).

Christianity means conflict. At the least, if it doesn't mean conflict, it certainly creates conflict! Unless we walk consistently in the Spirit, living holy is difficult. No, it is impossible! It isn't natural to "love your enemies and pray for those who persecute you" (Matthew 5:44 NASB). Forgiveness isn't natural. Without God it can't be done! We often talk about how God saved us from sin. I agree. I am grateful for the wicked things He saved me from. Because I was saved, I stopped committing those wicked sins. He set up a protest in my heart! He brought my trembling soul to His bleeding side and cleansed my very imaginations, intentions, and ambitions.

✤ I thank You, God, that You groan and protest my sinful behavior so I can then...

✤ With each of God's challenges to my proclivities, I can decide whether or not to...

From Superficial to Supernatural

> *The war between the house of Saul and the house of David lasted a long time. David grew stronger and stronger, while the house of Saul grew weaker and weaker* (2 Samuel 3:1 NIV).

Transformation is a process! It takes faith and patience to see the results that bring out the true nature of Christ in any of us. When we strip away the facade of the superficial and ask God to bring about the supernatural, we experience the real power of God. God wants to transport us from the superficial to the supernatural!

🌿 When I let go of the masks I wear—at church, my workplace, when I'm with family, when out with friends, etc.—and am authentic, the true nature of Christ in me can…

🌿 An example of the real power of God revealed through me is when He…

Liberty

> *Stand fast therefore in the liberty by which Christ has made us free, and do not be entangled again with a yoke of bondage* (Galatians 5:1 NKJV).

The blood of Jesus is efficacious, cleansing those who feel unclean. How can we reject what He has cleansed and made whole? Just as He said to the woman then, He proclaims today, "Neither do I condemn you; go and sin no more" (John 8:11 NKJV). How can the Church do any less? The chains that bind are often from events that we have no control over. The woman who is abused is not responsible for the horrible events that happened in her past. Other times the chains are there because we have willfully lived lives that bring bondage and pain. Regardless of the source, Jesus comes to set us free and bless us. He is unleashing His Church. He forgives, heals, and restores. All children of God can find the potential of their future because of His wonderful power operating in their lives.

🌿 Thank You, Jesus, that You came to set me free from...

🐦 Jesus, I welcome the liberty You provided for me when You…

Walking Wounded

> *The teachers of the law and the Pharisees brought in a*
> *woman caught in adultery. They made her stand before*
> *the group and said to Jesus, "Teacher, this woman was*
> *caught in the act of adultery"* (John 8:3-4 NIV).

Have you ever wondered where the man was who had been committing adultery with this woman? She had been caught in the very act. Surely they knew who the man was. There still seems to be a double standard today when it comes to sexual sin. Often we look down on a woman because of her past but overlook who she is now. Jesus, however, knew the power of a second chance. Some today are very much like this woman. Perhaps they have made strong commitments to Christ and have the very Spirit of God living within them, yet they walk as cripples, having been stoned and ridiculed. They may not be physically broken, but they are wounded within. The Church must throw off condemnation and give life and healing.

🌿 I am or I know of women who are still carrying scars from the past. What can I do to help them?

🌿 How can I encourage my church to pay special attention to all who walk through the doors with wounds still seeping?

Pleasure and Pain

Therefore we do not lose heart. Though outwardly we are wasting away, yet inwardly we are being renewed day by day. For our light and momentary troubles are achieving for us an eternal glory that far outweighs them all (2 Corinthians 4:16-17 NIV).

We went through a phase once when we thought real faith meant having no feelings. Now I believe that life without feelings is like a riverbed without water. The water is what makes the river a place of activity and life. You don't want to destroy the water, but you do need to control it. Feelings that are out of control are like the floodwaters of a river. The gushing currents of boisterous waters over their banks can bring death and destruction. They must be held at bay by restrictions and limitations. Although we don't want to be controlled by feelings, we must have access to our emotions. We need to allow ourselves the pleasure and pain of life.

🌿 The older I get, the more I feel like my body is "wasting away"— yet I feel my spiritual self is growing stronger—especially when I…

🌿 My feelings are usually under control, but watch out when…

Dying Body, Renewed Spirit

That is why we never give up. Though our bodies are dying, our spirits are being renewed every day. For our present troubles are small and won't last very long. Yet they produce for us a glory that vastly outweighs them and will last forever! (2 Corinthians 4:16-17 NLT).

Emotional pain is to the spirit what physical pain is to the body. Pain warns us that something is out of order and may require attention; something is not healed. In the same way, when pain fills our heart, there is an area where healing or restoration is needed. We dare not ignore these signals—or let them control us. Above all, we must allow the Spirit of God to counsel and guide us through the challenges of realignment when upheavals occur. Even the finest limousine requires tune-ups or realignments. There is a difference between minor and major adjustments. Removing someone from our lives is painful but not a major adjustment. People are born and die every day. They come and go, marry and divorce, get promoted and demoted. You can survive the loss of people, but you can't survive without God! He is the Force that allows you to overcome when people have taken you under!

🌱 Right now I know someone who really isn't a positive influence in my life and I should…

🦋 Am I a positive influence in my family, circle of friends, my church?

Beyond Loneliness

But Jesus often withdrew to lonely places and prayed (Luke 5:16 NIV).

God did most of His work on creation with no one around to applaud His accomplishments. So He praised Himself, seeing that "it was good." Have you stopped to appreciate what God has allowed you to accomplish, or have you been too busy trying to impress someone? No one paints for the blind or sings for the deaf. Their level of appreciation is hindered by their physical limitations. Although they may be fine connoisseurs in some other arena, they will never appreciate what they can't detect. Let's clap and cheer for the people whose absence teaches us the gift of being alone. Somewhere beyond loneliness there is contentment, and contentment is born out of necessity. It springs up in the hum of the heart that lives in an empty house, and in the smirk and smile that come on the face of a person who is amused with their own thoughts.

❧ When I am alone, I feel…

❧ Being alone doesn't always mean I'm lonely because…

Enjoy Yourself

Furthermore, because we are united with Christ, we have received an inheritance from God, for he chose us in advance, and he makes everything work out according to his plan (Ephesians 1:11 NLT).

Have you reached that place in life where you enjoy your own company? Have you taken the time to enjoy your own personhood? Have you massaged lotion into your own skin, or set the dinner table for yourself? Drive yourself to the mall and spend an afternoon picking out a gift for yourself. When you speak comfort and blessings to yourself, it reflects your own opinion about yourself. There are reasons to give yourself a standing ovation. The first is the fact that your steps are carefully observed and arranged by God Himself and are designed to achieve a special purpose in your life. People come and go during your life, and you are blessed either way (see Deuteronomy 28:6). Your blessing is not predicated on someone else. Rejoice because you are in step with the beat of Heaven and the purposes of God.

🌿 My inheritance from God includes:

🌿 This weekend I'm going to take time to enjoy myself by counting my blessings and then…

The Lord's Doing

> Then Jesus asked them, "Didn't you ever read this in
> the Scriptures? 'The stone that the builders rejected has
> now become the cornerstone. This is the Lord's doing,
> and it is wonderful to see'" (Matthew 21:42 NLT).

Jesus concluded that the rejections of men He experienced were the doings of the Lord! As Joseph so aptly put it, "You intended to harm me, but God intended it all for good. He brought me to this position so I could save the lives of many people" (Genesis 50:20 NLT). The Lord orchestrates what the enemy does and makes it accomplish His purpose in your life. How many times have "evil" things happened in your life that later you realized were necessary? If I hadn't faced trials like these, I wouldn't have been ready for the blessings I now enjoy. In the hands of God, even our most painful circumstances become marvelous in our eyes! When we see how perfectly God has constructed His plan, we can laugh in the face of failure. However, rejection is only marvelous in the eyes of someone whose heart has wholly trusted in the Lord!

❦ Have I wholly trusted in the Lord?

❦ Or am I grieving over something that someone has done—as though I have no God to direct it and no grace to correct it?

Still Standing

Watch, stand fast in the faith, be brave, be strong (1 Corinthians 16:13 NKJV).

God is in control, and what He has allowed, no one can disallow! If He said He was going to bless you, then disregard the mess and believe the God who cannot lie. The rubbish can be cleared and the bruises healed. Just be sure that when the smoke clears, you are still standing. You are too important to the purpose of God to be destroyed by a situation meant to give you character and direction. No matter how painful, devastated, or disappointed you may feel, you are still here. Praise God, He will use the cornerstone developed through rejections and failed relationships to perfect what He has prepared! Pull yourself up—it could have killed you, but it didn't. Announce, "I am alive. I can laugh. I can cry, and by God's grace, I can survive!"

🌿 It's very common for me to immediately panic when something goes wrong; rather, I should…

🌿 By God's grace I can survive, which means I will begin today to…

Teachers Young and Old

Likewise, teach the older women to be reverent in the way they live, not to be slanderers or addicted to much wine, but to teach what is good. Then they can urge the younger women to love their husbands and children (Titus 2:3-4 NIV).

Elisabeth, the wife of the priest Zacharias, is the biblical synonym for the modern pastor's wife. She was a winter woman with a summer experience. She was pregnant with a promise. In spite of her declining years, she was fulfilling more destiny then than she had in her youth. She is biblical proof that God blesses us in His own time and on His own terms. Many times when an older woman is still vibrant and productive it can cause jealousy and intimidation. Whatever the reason, Elisabeth was a recluse for six months until she heard a knock at the door. If you have isolated yourself from others, regardless of the reason, I pray you will hear the knocking of the Lord. He will give you the garment of praise to clothe the spirit of heaviness (see Isaiah 61:3).

🌿 I am younger than some and realize that the wisdom of older people in my life can...

I am older than some and realize the wisdom of sharing what I have learned, so…

Alone with God

The nations will see your righteousness. World leaders will be blinded by your glory. And you will be given a new name by the Lord's own mouth (Isaiah 62:2 NLT).

Jacob, whose name meant "supplanter" or "trickster," literally "con man," was left alone with God. God cannot accomplish anything with us until we are left alone with Him. In the isolation of our internal strife, God begins the process of transforming disgrace into grace. It only took a midnight rendezvous with God to bring Jacob's leg to a limp and his fist to a hand clasped in prayer. "I won't let You go unless You bless me," Jacob cries. God then tells Jacob he is really Israel, a prince (see Genesis 32:24-30). My friend, when we seek to know God, He will show us our real identity. The greatest riches Jacob received were given while he was alone with the Father—simply hearing his new name! You could be royalty and not know it. My friend, if no one else knows who you are, God knows.

✿ When I am alone with God…

✿ Would I wrestle with God if given the opportunity?

Not Defeated

> *I pray that your hearts will be flooded with light so that you can understand the confident hope he has given to those he called—his holy people who are his rich and glorious inheritance* (Ephesians 1:18 NLT).

Open your mouth and speak something good about yourself so you can stand up on your feet. You used your mouth against yourself. Then you spoke against people around you because you treated them like you treated yourself. Open your mouth now and begin to speak deliverance and power. You are not defeated. You are a child of God. When you start speaking correctly, God will give you what you say. Jesus tells us, "If you believe, you will receive whatever you ask for in prayer" (Matthew 21:22 NIV). God willed you something. Your Father left you an inheritance. God blessed the children of Abraham; surely He will bless His own child—you.

🌿 No one on earth has left me an inheritance, so this whole concept is…

🌿 I have received an inheritance from a relative and it made me feel…

Like Children

One day some parents brought their children to Jesus so he could touch and bless them. But the disciples scolded the parents for bothering him. When Jesus saw what was happening, he was angry with his disciples. He said to them, "Let the children come to me. Don't stop them! For the Kingdom of God belongs to those who are like these children. I tell you the truth, anyone who doesn't receive the Kingdom of God like a child will never enter it." Then he took the children in his arms and placed his hands on their heads and blessed them (Mark 10:13-16 NLT).

I am concerned that we maintain our compassion. How can we be in the presence of a loving God and then not love little ones? When Jesus blessed the children, He challenged the adults to become as children. Oh, to be a child again, to allow ourselves the kind of relationship with God that we may have missed as a child. Sometimes we need to allow the Lord to adjust the damaged places of our past. I am glad to say that God provides arms that allow grown children to climb up like children and be nurtured through the tragedies of early days. Isn't it nice to toddle into the presence of God and let Him hold you in His arms? In God, we can become children again.

🌿 My unhappiest childhood memory is:

My most happiest childhood memory is:

God's Intervention

God did this so that, by two unchangeable things in which it is impossible for God to lie, we who have fled to take hold of the hope set before us may be greatly encouraged (Hebrews 6:18 NIV).

Reach out and embrace the fact that God has been watching over you all of your life. My friend, He covers you, He clothes you, and He blesses you! Rejoice in Him in spite of the broken places. God's grace is sufficient for your needs and your scars. He will anoint you with oil. The anointing of the Lord be upon you now—bathing, healing, and strengthening as never before. There will be a time in your life when God nurtures you through a crisis situation. You may not even realize how many times God has intervened to relieve the tensions and stresses of day-to-day living. Every now and then He does us a favor—something we didn't earn or can't even explain, except as the loving hand of God. Many times He moves just in the nick of time—or so it seems to us. You can count on it!

🌿 I wish I could say I never lie—sometimes it just…

🌿 I can absolutely believe that God has intervened in situations when I thought all was lost; for example…

The Greatest Blessings

You say, "I am rich; I have acquired wealth and do not need a thing." But you do not realize that you are wretched, pitiful, poor, blind and naked (Revelation 3:17 NIV).

If you have ever sunkn down into the rich lather of a real covenant relationship, you are wealthy. This relationship is the wealth that causes street people to smile in the rain and laugh in the snow. They have no coats to warm them; their only flame is the friendship of someone who relates to the plight of daily living. In this regard, many wealthy people are impoverished. They have things, but they lack camaraderie. The greatest blessings are often void of expense, yet they provide memories that enrich the credibility of life's dreary existence.

❧ When I think of the greatest "free" blessing, what comes to mind is…

❧ I have/have not experienced the "rich lather of a real covenant relationship" with someone here on earth. _____

❧ But I do experience the "rich lather of a real covenant relationship" with Someone in Heaven every time I…

Bloody Tears

It is good for me that I have been afflicted, that I may learn Your statutes (Psalm 119:71 NKJV).

The bleeding trail of broken hearts and wounded relationships ultimately leads us to the richness of God's purpose in us. Periodically each of us will hear a knock on the door. It is the knock of our old friend Judas, whose cold kiss and calloused heart usher us into the will of God. To be sure, these betrayals call bloody tears to our eyes and nail us to a cold cross. Nevertheless, the sweet kiss of betrayal can never abort the precious promises of God in our life! The challenge is to sit at the table with Judas on one side and John on the other, and to treat one no differently from the other, even though we are distinctly aware of each one's identity and agenda. If you have been betrayed or wounded by some you brought too close, please forgive them. They really were a blessing. You will only be better when you cease to be bitter!

🌿 Yes, this section reminds me of a few people who hurt me—and I choose right now to forgive and forget _____ and _____ and _____.

🌿 I will search my memory about the incidents and look for how God used those hurts to make me stronger and:

Conquer the Enemy Within

The Lord of hosts has sworn, saying, "Surely, as I have thought, so it shall come to pass, and as I have purposed, so it shall stand" (Isaiah 14:24 NKJV).

God creates by speaking, and He speaks out of His own thoughts. Since God's Word says, "...whatever is in your heart determines what you say" (Matthew 12:34 NLT), then we must go beyond the mouth to bring correction to the words we speak. We have to begin with the thoughts we think. I pray that somehow the Spirit will reveal the areas where you need Him to heal your thinking so you can possess the blessings God wants you to have. Then you will be able to fully enjoy what He has already given you. Many people have the blessing and still don't enjoy it because they conquered every foe—except the enemy within!

🌿 Sometimes my thoughts are so messed up that I think I'm going to...

🌿 Holy Spirit, please show me how to heal my thinking so I can...

Not a Dead Dog

> *"Don't be afraid," David said to him, "for I will surely show you kindness for the sake of your father Jonathan. I will restore to you all the land that belonged to your grandfather Saul, and you will always eat at my table." Mephibosheth bowed down and said, "What is your servant, that you should notice a dead dog like me?"* (2 Samuel 9:7-8 NIV).

Perception is everything. Mephibosheth thought of himself as a dead dog, so he lay on the floor like one. I feel a word going out from the Lord to you: You have been on the floor long enough! It is time for a resurrection, and it is going to start in your mind. Has God blessed you with something you are afraid of losing? Could it be that you think you are going to lose it because you don't feel worthy? I realize that living in the palace can be a real shock to someone who is accustomed to being rejected and ostracized. Without realizing it, you will accept being treated as though you were a dog. Mephibosheth had been through so much that he began to think himself a dead dog.

🌿 Sometimes I feel unworthy of God's blessings because:

🌿 And sometimes I confuse humbleness with self-condemnation, which causes me to:

Receive Your Blessing!

You will receive this blessing if you are careful to obey all the commands of the Lord your God that I am giving you today (Deuteronomy 15:5 NLT).

If you don't have sufficient passion, you will never have the force to overcome limitations and satanic restrictions. Power emerges from the heart of people who are relentlessly driven toward a goal. Desire is kindled in the furnace of need—an unfulfilled need. It is a need that refuses to be placated and a need that will not be silent. Many people who set out to accomplish goals are so easily discouraged or intimidated by their own anxieties that they relinquish their right to fight for their dreams. However, if there is a tenacious, burning desire in the pit of your stomach, you become very difficult to discourage. The crux of the matter is basically: How badly do you want to be blessed? How committed are you to sharing your blessings with others? Think and pray into this today.

🌱 Very good questions—just how badly do I really want to be blessed?

How careful am I to obey God's commands—willing enough to receive His blessings?

About the Author

Bishop T.D. Jakes has reached millions of people from all socio-economic backgrounds, races, nationalities, and creeds. Digital media, film, and television, among others, have been instrumental in helping Bishop Jakes meet the desperate needs of countless individuals. For more than 40 years, Bishop T.D. Jakes has helped millions of people realize their purpose through his dynamic ministry.

Recognized as "America's Best Preacher" by *Time* magazine, as well as "One of the Nation's Most Influential & Mesmerizing Preachers" by *The New York Times*, Bishop Jakes is a charismatic, yet humble man. In 1996, with minimal resources, T.D. Jakes founded The Potter's House (TPH) in Dallas, Texas, a non-denominational, multicultural church that grew to become a megachurch and global humanitarian organization.

He and his wife, Serita, have been married for more than 35 years and have five children and several grandchildren. Whether enjoying a long, relaxing walk along the beach or launching a business, T.D. and Serita Jakes support each other with their faith in God, and in each other.

From

T.D. Jakes

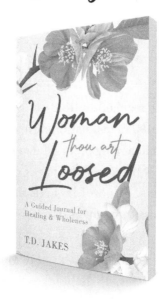

A unique, guided journaling experience

More than a blank page journal or fill-in-the-blanks exercise, this guided journal from Bishop T.D. Jakes provides a unique format for readers to explore their hearts, minds, desires, needs, wants, and spirits to manage their everyday lives, leading to an exciting lifestyle of health and happiness.

After reading specially selected excerpts from T.D. Jakes' bestselling books, readers are prompted with comments, scenarios, and questions designed to identify and/or stir up energies and emotions, secrets and situations that may be holding them back from experiencing freedom spiritually, physically, relationally, mentally, and emotionally.

With Scripture and inspirational writings by T.D. Jakes, readers can partner with the Holy Spirit to seek and find solace, joy, strength, and liberty. The journal focuses specifically on the uniquely personal aspects of womenÕs issues, and is designed to inspire and edify every reader to ponder her private dreams, yearnings, ideas, and musings.

Purchase your copy wherever books are sold

From

T.D. Jakes

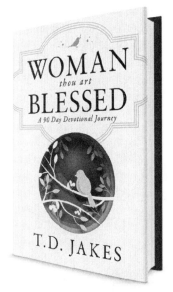

No matter your circumstances, God calls you blessed!

While you may not be able to control the unexpected trials and troubles you face on a daily basis, you can learn how to draw strength from the blessing of the Lord!

In his dynamic style, Bishop T.D. Jakes presents encouraging devotionals that help you boldly declare *"Woman, Thou Art Blessed!"* over every circumstance.

Over the next 90 days, immerse yourself in biblical truths about your blessed identity. Each devotional entry includes powerful declarations of blessing to help you confess and declare what God says about you—that you are deeply loved, highly favored and radically blessed.

When you see yourself the way God does, you can live the abundant life that Jesus promised!

Purchase your copy wherever books are sold

From

T.D. Jakes

Experience Freedom from the Pain of Your Past!

Many women are not enjoying an abundant, full and satisfying life because they are still *imprisoned* to the *pain of the past*. **It's time to get free... and live free!**

In *Woman, Thou Art Healed and Whole*, Bishop TD Jakes shares words of encouragement that will heal your soul and liberate your heart.

So what is holding you back from living life to the fullest?

Maybe you have experienced trauma, abuse, destructive relationships, betrayal, pain from poor decisions, unforgiveness, guilt or shame. These prisons are constantly looking for souls to claim and restrain.

Even though you may have already received God's forgiveness, it's time for you to start walking in the **healing** and **wholeness** He has made available to you.

Get ready to experience Heaven's healing for your past so you can start enjoying the abundant life *today!*

Purchase your copy wherever books are sold